The 6 Keys to 6 Figures

And Overall Financial Prosperity in the 21st Century

Theodore E. Renka

Theodore E. Renka

Printed in the United States of America

First Printing: 2018

ISBN- 9781791324636

A quick note from the Author

A couple quick things before you start your journey to Six-Figures!

First, if after reading this book, making some changes, and taking action as outlined in these pages, you feel that you still could use some more help achieving your Six-Figure goals, feel free to reach out to me at theodoreerenka@yahoo.com. This is an e-mail I set up for my readers to contact me if needed.

Some areas I have helped people in are:

-Motivation

-Discipline

-Efficiency

-Positivity

-Writing

-Sales Training

-Wellness

-Brainstorming

-Business Consulting

And the list goes on.

One of my true passions in life has become helping people. Since publishing this book the demand for my coaching, mentoring, or whatever term we would like to call it has been tremendous. As a result, I implore you to really dig into the content in this book and see how far you can take it on your own. However, if you do hit a wall and need help, I am here for you.

Secondly, I remember reading a book and the author had a page asking for 5-star Amazon reviews and I thought it was strange to say the least. Then I wrote a book and I completely understand! The reason being is not all reviews make it online, and without reviews flowing in the Amazon algorithm will show your book to shoppers less. So, if you like the book or you feel it could help others please take a moment to go to Amazon and post a 5 star review so we can make as many Six-Figure earners as possible!

CONTENTS

FOREWORD

Congratulations! Why am I congratulating you? I do this because you opened this book and began reading it. You have already done more than the vast majority of people in this world do for themselves. By buying this book you are investing in yourself, your future, and the generations to come. The investment required is more of an investment of time and effort than of money, but the time and effort required is most likely little more than what you do now to earn whatever you are earning. It will just be time and effort better spent, with more direction and focus on the correct things. Things that will get you toward your goal of a six-figure income.

Ahhhh… the coveted six-figure income. With the median individual income in the United States of America being around $28,000 at the time I'm writing this book, there are many people wishing and dreaming of a six-figure income. They are dreaming of a big house, sports car, or jewelry. Or perhaps they are dreaming of more freedom, things they could do with their families, and financial security. There are many things that are possible with a six-figure income. The fact of the matter is, I don't care *why* you and so many others want a six-figure income, I just want to help you get it!

I'm going to paint a little picture for you about the moment I got the motivation to write this book, and some of the things I'm about to say may sound a little ostentatious. This is not done for bragging purposes what so ever. Not one bit. This is done so you can perhaps see and feel my motivation for writing this. I was sitting beside my pool in the backyard of my primary home. I say primary because at the time I owned five homes. It is my dream home—three thousand square feet plus a finished basement complete with a game room, bar, and a gym. I was staring at the view across the valley and the other mountains, at the clouds rolling by, soaking up the sun as I usually do on a hot summer day. As I lay there a feeling of absolute gratitude rolled over me like a tank.

I thought to myself, "This is the life I dreamed about." Then a totally different feeling engulfed me. "Is this a dream? Am I going to wake up from this as a kid, broke and alone?" Obviously, I didn't wake up. This is my life. The life I heard about people living growing up but never experienced it firsthand. The life of abundance, love, freedom, and gratitude. Right then I decided that I had to help as many people get here as possible. How could I do that? What is the best and most efficient way to help as many people as possible live the life of their dreams, the life they deserve? I thought about a bunch of different ways, but none seemed as effective as writing a book. So here we are.

Now, I want to tell you a little about me, so you know I am qualified to educate on this subject. There are two types of authors who write self-help books. The first kind I will call the researchers. These authors research a topic heavily, gather huge amounts of facts, and then write a book on their findings. The second type is the people who are speaking from their own experience. The latter is who I am. These people have done it, lived it, and are now telling about it. I can't say one is better than the other. Both can provide great advice and education.

I have the experience. I did not grow up in a six-figure household. Not by a long shot. My mother and father separated when I was three. My mother was a bookkeeper and my father a teacher. There were many lean years, and there was never extra. I saw what financial pressures did to my mother. She was often very stressed and always worried about money. I had a great father and he did more than what was required, but he had his own bills to pay. There were plenty of years where we had no television because the old one broke. Or I had to borrow a bike from someone in the neighborhood because I didn't have my own. I would have to go over my friend's house to play video games as we didn't have any. I am not complaining as I know that many have it far worse, but I didn't come from money.

Growing up having these money problems lit a fire in me. I always looked for ways to make money. I would look through magazines and dream of being able to buy some of the things I saw. When I graduated high school, I didn't know what I wanted to do, but I knew I wasn't going to college. I wanted one thing and one thing only—to make money. I went through twelve years of school, learned everything they taught me, passed all their tests, and had no idea what to do to make some money! So I tried to get into the military like my father and uncles did, but couldn't due to health and legal issues (I was a little wild when I was a kid). A year after I graduated high school my mom thought it was time for me to be on my own, so at 19 I moved from New Jersey to sunny Florida.

I got a sales job on the west coast of Florida. When I was 20 years old I had my first five-figure month. By the time I was 22 years old I was running my own sales team of 10 sales people making six figures. I had a brand new Rolex, fishing boat, big four-bedroom house with an in-ground pool on a lake, and a bright green Ninja motorcycle. Now I am 33, I manage a team of 18 sales people and four sales managers, and I own and run my own real estate investing business. My income is, and has been, well into the six figures.

I tell you all this for two reasons. First, to show you success is possible from humble beginnings. Second, that I didn't invent something or have some brilliant idea that made me insanely rich. My approach to the success we are aiming for in this book is very organic, very grass roots. In other words, almost anyone can do it. I don't have some genius brain power, nor was I born with some incredible work ethic. I am a normal guy from New Jersey who put some effort into being the best I can be. Moreover, another reason why I feel this book will be so effective is that I am not some loud fast-talking multi-millionaire. I am very accessible, approachable, heck I could be your neighbor! Yet my income is in the top 5% in the United States.

I have done it. I have helped others do it. Now you will do it. Open your mind, allow yourself to not just read, but absorb and digest the information I am about to give you. Sometimes words aren't enough, so throughout this book I will give you 'actionable' advice. Too often books have a lot of nice ideas, thoughts, and information but lack one of the most important pieces: how can I use this now? I'm talking about actions and habits you can introduce into your life to make an immediate and long-lasting change for the better. To bring your life to the next level. We will call these **AAA's**, for Actionable Advice Alerts.

Some of it may make sense to you, some of it may sound a little weird or crazy. But maybe it will take something a little weird and crazy to get you there, especially if what you're doing now isn't. Thanks for getting this book, for investing in yourself. I sincerely, from the bottom of my heart hope that this helps you and many others. Being blessed with the type of life I live I felt it was my duty to help others do the same. So with that said, let's begin...

KEY #1

The Six Figure Mindset

Perhaps you have heard about the importance of having the correct mindset. Maybe from a friend, or a mentor, or even a professional speaker. Some people might talk about having a positive or negative mindset. Using this as the first "key" is no accident. Out of the six keys it is by far the absolute most important. Why is mindset so important? First let's look at the definition: "an attitude, disposition, or mood." Thinking of it in this way, that means everything we encounter all day long will be interpreted through the lens of our mindset—things that happen to us, that are said to or around us, the traffic on the way to work, the weather.

Let me give you an example.

What is the first thing most of us encounter every day? Getting out of bed. Let's say you must get up at 6am for work. Your mindset could be frustration: "How is it 6am already? Ugh, I have to go to work now!" Or it could be motivational: "It's time to get up! I **GET** to go to work now!" I know what you're thinking, that it's not that easy, or that you're not a morning person. I'm with you, you're right! It's not that easy, and most of us aren't! However, you are reading this book to learn the six keys to six figures, and the first step is to gain the proper mindset. If you commit to practicing this and the other keys you will achieve this mindset, and much, much more.

AAA: Tomorrow morning when that alarm clock goes off, instead of saying "I have to go to work now," make a small change and say to yourself, "I *get* to go to work now." It may seem like a simple idea that couldn't possibly alter anything, but understand that your mind is a very powerful tool, and when you say "I get to go to work now," instead of "I have to go to work now," your brain immediately thinks of reasons why you are so lucky that you get to go to work! It's amazing! Instead of thinking about why you have to go to work, such as, 'the bills have to get paid', or 'I need the health insurance', your brain thinks, 'I could be one of those out of work people on the news', or 'imagine if I didn't have the health insurance from my job when I got sick last year'. A whole new perspective just from changing that one thought. Now, is it always going to make you leap out of bed with joy? Probably not, but at the very least it will start your day on a grateful, uplifting note as opposed to a sad, frustrated one.

By studying this book and using these lessons you will get to the point where you are constantly being asked by your friends, family, and co-workers, "How are you always so positive?" Or they will say, "I wish I was more like you, you're so lucky." People will look at you with envy, or in awe, because with the proper mindset everything seems to roll right off your back. You know problems are going to come, so when they do you attack and solve them as opposed to dismissing them or putting them on the back burner. Have you ever seen someone and thought, "That person really has it together." Do you believe he or she was born that way? Not likely.

It is a deeply rooted belief that your mindset is what it is, that the way you interpret or react to events you see or hear is ingrained in you and cannot be changed. That is absolutely not the case. We humans have the unique ability to choose how we act, think, and conduct ourselves. When we learn to harness that ability and mold it into who or what we want to become, the outcome is astounding. How else do you explain some people with terminal illnesses being upbeat and happy? Or someone wrongfully imprisoned for 20 years being grateful and inspiring? That is a matter of choice. They chose to be that way by molding their way of thinking, their mindset. Think of your mindset as pottery on a wheel. It starts out as a big glob of mud. When the potter gets it turning on that wheel, it doesn't all happen at once. It takes some work, and some time, with some persistence it starts to take shape until finally, before you know it you have a beautiful piece of pottery that if taken care of will serve you for a lifetime.

The same idea applies to developing your mindset. You can try to learn how to do it yourself, and you might get there eventually, or you can follow the teachings in this chapter to guarantee victory and success! This is **ACTIONABLE** advice that anyone can do, and when executed it will make immediate improvements on your mindset and therefore your life. Let yourself be excited. Start to think of the possibilities in your life when you see that glass as half full instead of half empty. Imagine yourself as that powerful, inspiring, impressive person you strive to be. Get ready. . . Dig in . . . And let's go!

Positivity

The first way to improve your mindset is positivity. Having a more positive outlook is something many people strive for. Why is it that sometimes we are in a great, happy, powerful mood, and other times we feel tired, weak, and constantly dwell on the bad? We will discuss exactly that in this section and I will show you ways to be more positive all the time.

A very important method to a more positive attitude is gratitude—being grateful for what you have now, today, at this very moment. Oprah Winfrey said, "Be thankful for what you have; you'll end up having more. If you concentrate on what you don't have, you will never, ever have enough." Here is a person that came from very humble and troubled beginnings who has flourished into a hugely successful and powerful person. Oprah had many difficulties in her life that were beyond her control that could have buried her in depression and self-loathing. Instead, she focused on the positive aspects of her life—though they may have been hard to find—and gained strength from those terrible events that could have crushed her.

Now some people may say, "But I don't have anything to be grateful for right now," or "I just lost everything! How can I be grateful?" We all have something to be grateful for. Do you live in a free country where you can aspire to be whatever you want? There are a lot of people born into countries that have hardly any freedom. Places that have few options or opportunities for their people. Were you born with two arms, and two legs, and a good functioning brain?

If so you're ahead of the game! That is great! Some people are born with all types of health issues, and some of these brave people do great things. If you are one of them, good for you! Do you have enough to eat and clean water to drink daily? If you do, perform a little research and see how many people in this world are starving every day and getting sick from drinking unclean water.

My point is we **ALL** have something to be grateful for.

AAA: Stop and take a few minutes to think of the things you are grateful for. Get to a comfortable position and close your eyes, take a few deep breaths deeply in and out, and then think of how lucky you are. Maybe you are grateful for your family, or your health, or your job, or some experiences you have had in life. Are you grateful for taking action and reading this book? Think about a happy, proud, exhilarating, moment in your life—getting a degree, a child being born, a triumph in sports, a sexual encounter, or a great night out with friends. Picture being there and enjoying it. You probably feel a little better already. That is a brief positivity meditation. Do this as much as you like or need to. Perhaps in the morning, or right before bed.

Remember to breathe deeply in through your nose and exhaling deeply out through your mouth when you are thinking about all the things your grateful for, and how lucky you are. Behaviors like this are what make people positive in this crazy world we live in. This practice can last a few minutes or up to a few hours. It's totally up to you and what gets you results.

The next turn on the road to being more positive is quite simple: **<u>AVOID NEGATIVITY!</u>** It sounds so simple, right? However most people are constantly force feeding themselves negativity and ruining their chances at being positive without even realizing it! It's not your fault, we are simply wired that way. A lot of our seemingly unexplainable behaviors actually originate in our caveman days. What was the number one goal back then? Survival. The ones that survived were the ones that focused on what could kill them—predatory animals, poisonous berries, falling off a tree or a cliff, etc. Back then if you closed your eyes and concentrated on how lucky you are and how great everything is, a sabretooth tiger would probably rip you to shreds! Now, since we no longer have to constantly worry about basic survival, we can rewire ourselves to focus on the <u>quality</u> of our survival.

Unfortunately there are industries that exploit that attraction to negativity we were born with. The largest and most damaging one being the news. Hear me out here, because if you are an avid news watcher like I used to be, you are naturally going to resist what I'm about to tell you. Why are there so many channels on television and the radio dedicated to news? Furthermore, why is everything on the news bad news? Nothing good happened today? Anywhere? I don't buy it! The truth of the matter is these news outlets are after one thing, and it's not a deep desire to bring you all the current events they can for the good of mankind. The only thing they are after is money. Have you ever seen the buildings of the big news channels near you? Chances are they are absolutely huge, beautiful, and in the most expensive real estate area around. These companies are raking in cash from other companies that want to advertise their products during the commercial breaks of the news programs. What gets these companies to give top dollar to the news channel? The best ratings of course. How does the news channel get the best ratings? By having the largest viewership, from showing and talking about the one thing that most people can't tune out of: negativity, in the form of wars, slander, and violence. There is an old saying in the reporting world, "If it bleeds, it leads". In other words, the more guts, gore, or fear, the better!

This is the first thing that people tune into in the morning and the last thing a lot of us do before bed. What is that doing to your brain? I'm going to go a little off topic here for a moment because it is important to know some basic functions of the brain to understand this section. This wonderful tool we were blessed with called the human brain is a sponge, and the subconscious is the a part of your brain that is always listening and working. Here is an example of a function of the subconscious. Have you ever had something you were trying to remember, like a name of a person or a title of a movie, 'on the tip of your tongue', but you couldn't remember it? Then a few hours later it pops into your head? That is your subconscious at work. While the other part of your brain, the conscious part, has stopped working on remembering that name, the subconscious has not. Then, like magic, when the subconscious recalls the name, it throws it up to the conscious brain and boom! You got it!

Isn't that amazing? Wouldn't it be great if you could harness the power that the subconscious possesses? I will show you how to do this later, but for now since we have a basic understanding of the brain's functions let's talk about what watching or listening to nonstop news does to us. When we think about those great positive thoughts we are force feeding our brain powerful, happy emotions. Therefore the subconscious receives those thoughts, focuses on them, and shoves them into our conscious mind, resulting in the happy, grateful mood and mindset we were after.

Conversely, when we use that same thought suggestion to force feed our brains with what is on the news repeatedly throughout the day, guess what happens. You got it, the subconscious focuses on the death, crime, and sadness that the news so often purveys. Nowadays, to make things worse, most news channels are biased to one agenda or another, so the stories they are talking about are distorted to further whatever political cause they back. Ugh! Am I telling you to stop watching the news altogether? No. I am however telling you to change the way you take in your news. Don't just wake up in the morning, or lie in bed at night, and tune into the news out of habit or boredom. Whatever issues interest you that you want an update on, get the update and get out! Personally, I don't watch or listen to the news. If there is some current event I want an update on I go to the news section on my phone, see what's up, and that's it. I resist the urge to scroll through the headlines because I know I won't find anything that will make my day better in there.

Now that you have a whole new perspective of the news, and you plan to avoid it as much as possible, think of all that free time you have. I'm talking about the time you would have spent watching news on television, or on your phone, or listening on the radio in the car. Maybe now that time could be spent with family, or exercising, or reading.

AAA: Avoid absorbing too much news! Don't fall for it anymore! You will be absolutely amazed at the results when you commit to this. You will find yourself focusing on better things, feeling happier, and having more energy. Don't allow yourself to be brainwashed anymore. It's a game changer.

Any other negativity you run into during your day must also be avoided. You need to have an alarm in your brain that goes off when it senses negativity. As soon as it goes off, get out of there! Is it your neighbor at the end of your driveway talking about the terror alert going up? Or a co-worker at the water cooler complaining about not getting a raise or being forced to work extra hours? You run into these situations all the time and don't even realize it. That changes now. Avoid it like you would avoid radiation. GET AWAY! You are or will become like the people you choose to associate yourself with, so please, associate with good, positive, uplifting people. That means that you may have to cut certain people out of your life. Or you may have to have a conversation with some of them saying you don't want to hear negativity anymore. Maybe you can even help them avoid negativity too and improve their lives!

Determination

Determination, persistence, grit, perseverance; whatever you want to call it, it is a vital part to a productive mindset. Calvin Coolidge, the 30th president of the United States, once said, "Nothing in the world can take the place of persistence. Talent will not; nothing is more common than unsuccessful men with talent." Why is this so important? Why do so many talk about persistence and constantly chase it? It is because life will constantly knock you down, and it will beat you more when you're down there if you let it. A lot of the shots you take throughout your life are failures. Perhaps a failed relationship, job opportunity, diet, business, or a host of other things. Not only is failure a part of life, but the more successful a person is, typically the more failures they have had. Yes, you read that correctly. It is said that Thomas Edison failed over 10,000 times at inventing the light bulb. Ten-thousand times! Henry Ford went bankrupt twice before his success with the Ford Motor Company. The list of successful people with many failures goes on forever. If you are afraid to fail, you will fail to succeed.

When the mindset I am speaking about is attained, failure is looked at as a learning opportunity, not a reason to give up. For instance, let's say you want to lose 20 lbs. You give yourself two months to do it. Two months go by and you only lost 10. Oh no! You didn't accomplish the 20 lbs.! Is it time to cancel your gym membership and eat two cheeseburgers? Of course not. You need to take a moment and analyze why the weight didn't melt away at the rate in which it was planned to. Perhaps your diet needs to be adjusted, or cardiovascular exercise needs to be increased and weight lifting decreased. Learn from the failure, that is how you get better.

Most people reading this book can relate to a failed relationship. Especially if it was an important person to you, that can be very painful. Some people in their despair vow to never get that emotionally involved with a person again to avoid ever feeling that hurt again. This, despite how hard the heartache may be, is a mistake. One of life's greatest pleasures is finding someone that you are compatible with, that you can spend time with, and who makes you a better person. If you failed at a relationship before and because of this you don't allow yourself this pleasure for the rest of your life, you are really missing out. Instead, lessons need to be learned from the failure. Did you two have different views on important issues? How about different values? Did one of you push the other away? What things can you do different to make the next one work? Perhaps you are attracting the wrong type of person in the first place.

The same technique must be applied to your life. Let's say you changed careers because you were unfulfilled for one reason or another. Perhaps your income was capped, or there was no more room for advancement. You try something completely different and fail. You don't enjoy it or the money didn't add up. Do you run back to your old job and give up? Or do you understand that perhaps you learned that job wasn't quite right for you and you must look for another. Perhaps you dream of owning your own business, and decide to open a restaurant. Then the restaurant doesn't do the business you projected and you must close the doors. Do you go back to the 9-5 and give up your dream? Or do you analyze why it didn't produce the capital needed to succeed? Was the type of food wrong for the area? Location bad? Figure out what went wrong, don't make the same mistake again, and push forward. That's what determination is about. When you get knocked down, brush yourself off and try again.

I know what some people are thinking when they read this. That's nice, but it's harder than it sounds. Who wants to keep failing? No one. However, there is something that helps you get through those tough times.

AAA: You must discover your <u>WHY</u>. What is your why? Why do you want to earn six figures a year? Why do you want to achieve any of your other goals? Too often we only think about <u>what</u> we need to do, when we should be thinking <u>why</u> we need to do it. Let me break it down. A 'what' is earning six figures. A 'why' is to be able to provide for your family above and beyond the basics. To be able to take nice vacations. To get a bigger house. Or maybe you want to start a foundation, give to charity, feed the homeless. Only you know what your why is. If you know right away what it is, great! If not, put some thought into it. It will be something that gives you great peace of mind, pride, happiness, or fulfillment.

Your 'why' must be very important to you because it is what is going to keep you going when the road gets bumpy. When you have to work those long hours, or when you have to get up at the crack of dawn day after day, or when all your friends are watching the big game and you have to work, or do research. <u>Work while they play, so you can live like they dream</u>. I heard someone say something to that effect once and it really hit home. It immediately made me think of all the parties I missed over the years. All the trips to the beach, and days going to sporting events. Ironically it didn't make me sad, it made me happy! It made me happy because I knew <u>why</u> I was working while my friends were playing. Looking back at the sacrifices I made to get to where I am and to where I'm going, I feel blessed. I feel so grateful I was blessed with the foresight to know I might be missing out on a good night, but I may be gaining an incredible life. As with attaining most great things, other things will have to be sacrificed. That is also when your why really gets put to use. It may be sacrificing time with friends or family, or sleep, or certain pastimes, but it must be done. Now don't think you have to throw these things away in total. In fact, I urge you in the opposite direction. I greatly encourage hobbies and having fun. You must have a balance in life to feel powerful and ready to take on the world. It can't be all business. They may just have to be cut back or juggled around to fit in to your new busy, productive, positive life.

Focus

Being able to properly focus is extremely important to achieving a successful mindset, especially in this world of distractions we live in. We practically have access to the world right at our fingertips through our smart phones. Movies, sports, shows, games, and much more are there for our enjoyment at any time we like. We have communication with friends or family, either by voice or even face to face, regardless of where you are. Then there is social media.

Where do I start? You can see what your friend had for breakfast, or who your ex is dating, or where your cousin is vacationing. Isn't that great? . . . Or is it? I think it is great, when used correctly.

See, all this technology is a gift and a curse. If you are constantly checking your social media, or watching your favorite TV series, or text messaging your friends instead of working, that would be the curse. Conversely, if this technology is used to learn, progress, and create, that is the gift. To be clear, I am not swearing off social media, or staying in contact with friends, or taking an occasional break and watching a video. We must have that balance. In fact giving your brain a brief break is very important to productivity, which we will learn more about later in this section.

But oh what a gift this technology is! All that learning available to you anytime. I get excited just thinking about it. Want to learn how to tile a floor, hang dry wall, or re-stain your dresser? How about invest for retirement, find a new career, or start a new business? Maybe you want to learn how to attract the opposite sex, be a better runner, or run for political office? The point is, this is the information age. Fifty years ago if you wanted to learn about home improvement, or IRAs, or different career paths, what did you do? Either ask around, and therefore trust whoever your find, (risky), or go to the library and try to find some books on the topic. Not today. Just start up that computer or turn on your phone, and boom! There it is. The Internet. All the information in the world there for you. What are you going to do with it?

Ever have those days when you think about all the things you have to do, and you get overwhelmed? Instead of starting to accomplish whatever tasks you have at hand, you just keep going over them in your head. It feels like there is a tornado in your brain.

AAA: Make a list. This simple little trick works for daily or longer term personal items, or business tasks, or both. That's it. Something magical happens when we write things down. All of a sudden you will feel more organized, and probably a little calmer and more confident. Plus, you get the bonus of scratching items off when they are completed. That will give you a feeling of accomplishment, which will in turn motivate you. The trick is to remember to do it. Next time you have a multitude of tasks, chores, appointments, or phone calls to do, make a list. Another tip, perhaps the most important rule to productivity, is to put the one you want to do the least, first. Get that conversation, or project, or whatever it is you are dreading, done with and gone. There are two reasons for that. When you have something hanging over your head you don't want to do, you don't do other things as well or with as much enthusiasm because your brain is thinking about still having to deal with that other task. Also, when you get the hardest item out of the way, all the other ones seem like a piece of cake!

As a side note, you will be reading the **AAA's** throughout the book. Some of these actions may seem too simple or easy to make a difference. The simplicity and ease of these actions is the point. Changing yourself to move toward that six-figure income is simple. Almost anyone can do it, so please, I implore you, don't just read these pieces of advice and move on. Put them into action, as much as you can. It is very important to your end goal of a six-figure income. Now, back to the art of focusing.

Another way to increase your focus is to limit your distractions. First, you must be conscious about how much you are distracted in the first place. I've had employees who I've told that they are on their phone too much and they look at me like I'm crazy. "I'm never on my phone!" they will say. Then I show them the surveillance camera footage and they are amazed. "Wow, I had no idea!" they will say, if they are honest. If not they will try to justify it, knowing they were in the wrong. The reason for this is, our phones, especially for the younger generations, have become like an extension of our hands. We often unconsciously pick them up and open our e-mail or the news feed, sometimes without even noticing it. You must take an honest look at your behavior, assess it, and make some changes. Perhaps limit using your phone to three times a day, except for phone calls and important texts. You need to get to a point where if you pick up your phone for no real reason you can catch yourself, realize you are about to be distracted, and put it down.

I am using the phone as an example, but it could be whatever distracts you. Maybe it's the home page of your Internet browser. That can easily get you lost in its pages of celebrity gossip, political goings on, and advertisements. Or maybe it's a window in front of your desk you gaze out of. Discover what distracts you, and either cut it out or limit it and your focus level will skyrocket!

Goal Setting

This section is probably the most fun of this chapter. It is titled 'goal setting' because that is the commonly used term for what we are going to speak about. I also call this act **'life planning'**. Imagine, actually planning your life so it turns out the way <u>you</u> want it to. Doesn't that sound exciting? It is exciting, and empowering, and once you do it and follow through, your life will NEVER be the same. Sure, life will throw you curve balls now and again, but with the right planning you will stay on track. This is the final section of the 'mindset' chapter, because when you put to use what you are going to learn in the following paragraphs, it will fuel more of what was spoken about in the previous sections. In other words, you will feel more positive, determined, and focused. The reason for this is the brain performs at a higher level when it has something to look forward to. For instance, how do you feel when you are about to go on vacation? You feel upbeat, happy, energetic, and therefore more productive and creative. The same thing happens when you set goals in the proper way.

Having goals you are constantly striving for is absolutely vital to success in life, and most importantly for this book, in reaching that six-figure income mark. It is said that having no goals is like having a bow and arrow with no target to shoot at. You can constantly shoot the arrow and it just lands where it lands. Nothing really gets accomplished.

Chances are you may have set goals for yourself at some point in your life. When you were a child maybe your goals were to get straight A's, hit a certain amount of home runs in baseball, or be prom king or queen. Sometimes you hit those goals and sometimes you don't. That, after all, is life, right? The difference is, after reading, studying, and learning how to execute my 'life planning', you will know what goals to set, what time frame they should be completed by, and how to increase your chance of achieving them. Let's dive in!

The first rule of 'life planning' is your goals must be written down. Writing is a very powerful tool. When something is written down as opposed to just thought about, it becomes real. It becomes a tangible item that can be used again and improved over time. Get a notebook or something to write your goals in that has plenty of room, because you will be writing them down many times. If goals are written down once, the notebook is closed and put away. It's better than not doing it at all, but nowhere near as effective as writing them repeatedly.

AAA: Ideally you will write your goals down in the morning before your day gets started, and at night before you go to bed. By writing them down in the morning you are actively telling your brain what to focus on during the day. Your day will have more purpose when you know you are working toward your goals. They are to be written again at night so your subconscious can focus on them while you sleep. Your brain will help you find ways to achieve your goals while you are sleeping; it's pretty cool!

Next, let's talk about time frame. Your goals should fall into one of three time frame categories: short term, medium term, and long term. A short term goal should be achievable from now up to six months. Medium term should be able to be completed in six months to two years. Then finally, long term is two years and beyond. Of course these terms are approximations because you will see some goals may border on short to medium, or medium to long. That is fine. Put them in a category and stick to it.

Initially, coming up with these goals is a lot of fun. What do you want to accomplish in six months? Find a new job? Get a promotion? Open a new business? Maybe save a certain dollar amount? How about invest a certain dollar amount? What about in two years? Buy an income property? Complete a training course for a higher paying position? How about 10 years? Perhaps having five different streams of income? Be financially independent? I am listing a lot of business goals because my purpose with this book is to show you how to get to six figures, but your personal goals should be in here to. Whatever you want to get accomplished should be in this list and reviewed constantly. Do you want to start a family? Lose weight? Do charity work? Whatever it is, write it down and start taking action immediately.

These goals need to become a healthy obsession. If they are written down and reviewed multiple times a day, they will be. Your brain will constantly look for ways to achieve your goals because you are forcing it to. You will shut out distracting noise and focus on only what you desire. It is like when you are hungry for a meal, all you can think about is what to eat and how to get it. Except now you will be hungry for the attainment of your goals. If you feel overwhelmed getting started, what do you do? Make a list. You want to get that training done so you can get the promotion? Then make a to-do list in the morning and on it should be 'sign up for training'. If buying an income property is a goal, then on your daily to-do list should be 'call realtor', or 'look at two houses'. You must get the ball rolling and keep it that way. A body in motion stays in motion. Keep pushing!

Both your goals and daily to-do items to reach your goals should be unambiguous. As an example, if you want to save money to open a business, a certain dollar amount must be listed. Perhaps the goal would be 'save $500 a month', and your daily to-do to help with that may be 'pack lunch' so you don't have to buy lunch at work. The goal can't be simply 'save money'. The brain needs something specific to work towards. If your goal was simply save money, you could save $5 and have achieved your goal, but that isn't going to get you much closer to opening that business.

You must be creative with this process and enjoy it. Visualize yourself achieving these goals. How does it feel? What do your friends and family think about your progress? Think of different ways to keep the goals in the forefront of your mind. Have your phone remind you twice a day of your goals. Think and talk about your goals on your commute to work. I do that a lot. Don't worry, you won't look like you're crazy, people will just think you're on the phone. Then, when you complete your first goal and scratch it off the list. . . What a feeling! You will feel so powerful and in control when you are planning your own life instead of just going wherever life takes you.

KEY #2

The Mind Body Connection

You have read through chapter one and have mastered the art of creating and maintaining a positive, determined, and focused mindset. Congratulations! Now we must give that finely tuned brain of yours a healthy, strong, and well cared for body to carry out your life plans. This chapter will speak about the importance of taking care of your physical self. You could have a fantastic mindset, but without a well-cared for body to carry you through life, achieving all that you desire will be difficult. Don't worry, I'm not speaking about having six pack abs, bench pressing 300 pounds, or running marathons. Not even close. However, the body can't be neglected either.

In today's age of computers, video games, face time phone calls, and many other convenience creations, we all find ourselves more sedentary. From children glued to computer screens and video games instead of going outside and riding bikes or playing sports, to adults picking up their phones and 'face timing' instead of going and visiting friends or family face to face, people spend less time being active. Plus, the old 40-hour workweek for a lot of us sounds like part-time compared to the 60-hour weeks many of us put in, limiting time for physical activity. Vast advancements in transportation options have opened up new opportunities for many, but have also lowered the amount of people who walk or bike to get around. This all leads to a huge obesity problem.

It's time to wake up! We can't keep getting fatter and sicker! We aren't running around the woods looking for shelter and food like our caveman days. We have supermarkets where we can get all the food we can afford, and safe, secure, durable places to live in. As a result we must make the effort to eat and exercise properly. Taking care of our body needs to be a part of life.

There have been huge advancements in plastic surgery as well, which doesn't help our health crisis. What do a lot of people do when they have excess body fat and hate the way they look and feel? They head over to the plastic surgeon. Get the extra fat sucked out of them and go right back to the same bad habits and slowly put the weight back on. We are headed down a slippery slope. When the body stores too much excess fat away it is telling you to lower your caloric intake and increase exercise to burn extra calories. We must listen to what our bodies are telling us, and make adjustments accordingly. The body is like a car engine. If properly maintained, it will run for many years, and serve you well. If neglected, it will give you problems early on and simply will not last.

This chapter will give you the information and tools you need and actionable advice you can put to use immediately to get the most out of your body and therefore your mind. The mind and the body are intimately connected. The mind tells the body what hurts and what feels good. They communicate fatigue, energy, strength, and weakness. Putting what you learn in this chapter into practice will change your life. You will feel less aches and pains, more energy and strength, and you will look healthier and more attractive!

Diet

I know what you're thinking: 'diet'! Oh no, here comes the advice to eat nuts and lettuce all day, or starve myself. Don't worry, a 'diet' is simply the food that a person habitually eats. One can have a healthy, unhealthy, vegetarian, good, bad, or any other kind of diet. What we are going to speak about is a diet that will help us achieve our goal, which is to get to a six-figure income! That's right, the correct diet can help you earn more money. Here's how.

The food and drink that a person ingests is the fuel the body uses to complete the tasks at hand. If the body has bad fuel, it performs poorly— bad fuel being fatty, sugar rich, heavily processed food. Just like if bad fuel is put in a car it will not accelerate as it should, it will sputter, and could get damaged. Improving your diet follows the 80/20 rule— it is about 80% mental, and 20% physical. It's about changing habits and making better choices. The reason it is so hard for a lot of people to make the needed changes to their eating habits is a lot of people tie food to emotions. Therein lies the mind body connection when it comes to diet. For some, eating their favorite foods makes them feel happy, or safe. Often these emotions are rooted in childhood. The farther back these eating habits originate the harder it is to change them, but it is possible.

I once heard the saying, 'eat to live, do not live to eat'. It has become another one of my mottos. In other words, realize that food is simply something that keeps us alive, nourishes us, and gives us energy. To begin to make changes to your diet you must first change how you look at food in the first place.

AAA: Next time you feel hungry, instead of asking yourself what you want to eat, ask instead: what is available to me that will nourish me the best? What will give me the energy I need? What will make me feel great and satisfied? When you do this, your brain looks for what is best to eat instead of what will fulfill whatever habits you have developed over the years.

Most people know what will nourish their bodies the best, but in case you're not too sure, let's list some good food choices. To be clear, I am not a dietitian, I am simply giving you some basic advice to improve your eating habits to add another rung in the ladder you are climbing to the success you desire. One can't go wrong with most fruits and vegetables. Leafy greens, carrots, broccoli, and mushrooms are some vegetable examples that are readily available and contain excellent vitamins and minerals to give you great energy. They are also rich in fiber which is very good for digestive system health. Apples, strawberries, and bananas, to name a few, are some great fruit choices that are very convenient to keep at your desk at work or at home. Some other healthy choices besides fruits and vegetables are lean meats, like chicken, pork, and beef. Like vegetables and fruits, meat has important vitamins and minerals, plus they are rich in protein. Protein is very important because it helps build and maintain muscle, gives you a ton of energy, and keeps you feeling full for a long time. You want to limit the red meat intake as it can be high in fat and cholesterol, but you can eat just about all the white meat chicken you want. A good variety of food choices makes this transition easier. Do some research, find some tasty, healthy recipes that use good quality choices like the ones listed above.

With good food choices in mind, it is important we also speak about what is not so good to eat. Some of the top culprits of obesity today are sugar and fried foods. Eating a lot of sugar leads to excess body fat and studies have shown it to lead to deadly diseases. There are some foods that are obvious offenders like candy, cakes, and cookies. However some are not so obvious. In fact the human body actually turns white breads into sugars during digestion. Common examples of this would be pasta and the dough in pizza. A fantastic way to make a huge impact to your health is to eliminate all the white breads you can and replace them with whole wheat choices. Whole wheat breads aren't as processed as white bread, therefore it takes longer for your body to break them down, hence they don't turn directly into glucose, so you get longer lasting energy from them. At first you will miss the taste, but before you know it you will become accustomed to it and not even miss the white breads. Now let's talk about fried foods. The oil that fried food is cooked in and therefore saturated by is high in fat, which will pack on the pounds and will leave you feeling sluggish. Some common examples would be french fries, all different kinds of fried meats, potato chips, and donuts.

Another important part of changing bad eating habits is to understand what eating behaviors get the body working best. Once again we will revert back to our caveman days, before grocery stores and restaurants. Back then we didn't have three big meals a day and dessert after. Conversely, we grazed more, eating a little here and a little there. In those times humans would eat what they found during the day, perhaps a couple apples, some berries, a small animal maybe. Now, I'm no anthropologist, but I hope you see my point. We were not like lions or alligators that can have a huge meal and not eat for weeks. Our bodies need constant nourishment to perform at their best. When one institutes that into their modern day lives the results are amazing. The body will not store as much fat, and it will not feel as bloated or weighed down. Eating smaller meals with more snacks in between will leave you feeling lighter, more energized, and motivated.

We all know that feeling after a huge meal of spaghetti and meatballs or something similar —we don't exactly want to jump up and hammer away at our to do lists and goals. I think a more accurate description of our desire after a huge meal is to lie on the couch! Why is that? The reason is the digestive system pulls the blood from other parts of the body to aid in digesting such a huge meal, which in turn makes you want to sleep. That is why the correct diet is so important to success. There are only 24 hours in a day, time cannot be wasted trying to stay awake digesting your last meal! Moreover, a very important tip is to never let yourself get too hungry. When we are really hungry we tend to make poor choices because the brain is in survival mode. Don't let that happen. Always have healthy snacks around you, like apples, bananas, or granola bars. That way if for some reason your meal is delayed you won't get famished.

AAA: Plan your meals whether you're going to work or not. When you put your meals together ahead of time you will make better choices on content and portion size compared to ordering when you are already hungry. If you plan what you are going to eat throughout the day you won't be tempted by the many unhealthy fast food choices that are available. Plus you will save a ton of money bringing your meals from home—it really adds up. In addition, you won't fall into the bad eating habits those around you might have.

Now to be clear, I'm not saying to never eat for taste only again. I would never suggest that, because eating is one of life's great pleasures. The key is to make eating for taste only the exception, not the norm. When this is done you will not only be much healthier and able to accomplish more, but also when you do 'cheat' and eat that cheeseburger or pizza, it will taste so much better! It will be a real treat! You will see how much different you feel after eating that compared to a healthy meal, and after you're done and trying not to pass out from a food coma it will remind you to stay away from that type of food as much as possible.

Food isn't our only problem when it comes to bad diet habits. What we drink is also very important. Today's wide variety of sugar-filled drinks is a major health problem. It got so bad that the government had to limit the amount of sugar in soft drinks. Even so, one can of soda can have 66 grams of sugar in it. That is over 16 tea spoons of sugar in one drink! It's hard to believe but it is true, and it's not just soda. Many other drinks are nearly or just as bad, like energy drinks and iced teas. You must start reading the nutrition labels on what you eat and drink. Becoming aware of what you are putting in your body is vital. We only get one body, we <u>must</u> take care of it. The human body also needs good clean water on a daily basis and lots of it. If you are a person who doesn't drink much water, just focusing on constantly sipping on water all day will make a huge change in your body.

Everywhere you look today there is a new diet guaranteeing massive fat loss, from meat-only diets to no meat at all diets. Then there is all juice diets and vegan choices. No two bodies are alike, therefore everyone will react slightly differently to all diets, but one thing that I know to be true is moderation is key. Too much of any one thing is not good. It is also very important to enjoy your food. Eat! Be merry! Just make the right choices and you will have all the motivation and energy you need to get out there and crush it!

Exercise

Another very important part of the mind body connection is exercise. We know it's important, we were even forced to do it in school. Millions of people flood to their nearest gym at the beginning of every new year because it is on the top of nearly all new year's resolution lists. It is a multi-billion dollar industry between the work out gear, equipment, and the facilities. Even our basic human nature admires physical fitness going back to our caveman days when the bigger and stronger you were and appeared, the less you would be thought of as prey and could better protect your loved ones. Modern medicine also tells us that a lack of physical activity leads to many different cardiovascular diseases and obesity. Last but not least, if you exercise regularly you will look and feel better!

Then why doesn't everyone workout? The common excuses are 'I don't have time', 'I work too much', 'I'm too busy', 'I'm not motivated', 'I'm too tired'. There are many different reasons for the lack of exercise in many people's lives today. However, the largest reason people never start working out regularly, or don't continue to, goes back to something we spoke about in chapter 1 in the goal setting section. It's their 'why'. One must have a strong, powerful, motivating why to forgo all the distractions that tug at their attention. It takes a lot of motivation to go to the gym after work when your co-workers are headed to the bar, or to put down the remote and go for a run on your day off. It's not easy to get up early in the morning to exercise and handle all of our daily responsibilities. You need an important reason to do so. Just wanting six pack abs, big biceps, or sexy legs sometimes isn't enough. For some it is, and that is great. For others it isn't, and they choose watching TV, or sleeping in.

There is hope if you are one of the latter examples. You must find your why. What is going to motivate you? Living a longer life? Attracting a future spouse? Being a good example of health for your kids? Do you have a health issue that could be improved with exercise? These are a few common examples that motivate people to exercise regularly. You <u>must</u> find your <u>why</u> that will keep you focused on your fitness goals to achieve them. If your body is unhealthy and rotting from lack of physical activity, it is difficult for your mind to be sharp and focused. Do some research on highly successful CEOs and business owners. The vast majority of them swear by regular exercise to keep their brains sharp, focused, and creative.

This section is not about running a marathon, or becoming a bodybuilder. In fact, studies show that just 30-45 minutes of exercise three days a week will make a huge impact, improving heart health, overall body function, and increasing metabolism. That is less than three hours out of the 168 in a week. Ideally one would incorporate a mixture of stretching, aerobic or cardio, and strength training to have a well rounded routine. There are many different stretching techniques to keep you flexible. One very popular choice is yoga. It's different poses and breathing techniques are great for flexibility, as well as strength, and it has a great calming effect to help cope with everyday stresses. Calisthenics are exercises that use one's own body weight to increase strength, such as push-ups, pull-ups, sit-ups, and squats. These are great as they improve strength without the need of much equipment. Running, swimming, and playing sports like basketball or racquetball are great examples of aerobic exercise. This type of activity will burn fat and keep your heart strong.

Most of us know that feeling of being refreshed, powerful, and motivated after a good workout. The reason for that is when the body is pushed it produces endorphins. These are basically feel good chemicals that are released by the brain, almost like a reward for exercising! Find the workout regimen that works best for you and your lifestyle. For some they must work out first thing in the morning because it gets their energy levels up, gets the brain firing on all cylinders, and perhaps most importantly, makes sure it gets done. For some, after work is what is best for them. That can be great to exercise the daily stresses away and can help you sleep better too. Many people enjoy working out every day while others prefer every other day. There is no one size fits all advice when it comes to your health.

However, one thing is for sure, you <u>must</u> make exercise not just something you should do, it must become a part of your life. It must become a habit, something that is done no matter what, something that when it is missed you do not feel right. Then it will be something you can enjoy and be proud of for the rest of your life.

AAA: Get out a pen and paper, make a schedule for the upcoming week, and pencil in your time for exercise. Make sure to be smart and realistic about it. If you haven't worked out for five years don't pencil in a ten-mile run. At first it may just be thirty minutes of walking. Listen to your body. You are doing this to build your body up, not to tear it apart.

As you keep exercising you will see and feel great results which will motivate you and keep you pushing forward. You will be amazed at the increased brain function right after a good workout. It's like your brain finally woke up! Moreover, when you exercise regularly you will actually have more energy throughout the day and therefore will get more accomplished. I know retirees that have begun an exercise regimen in their retirement years because the doctor prescribed it for health issues. Before long they say they really enjoy it, and some have told me they regret not doing it their whole lives. They almost feel foolish knowing they would be healthier now and live longer. Don't let that happen to you. Don't be reactive and wait to do it when you have to—be proactive and start now! Finally, when you look and feel better, and are stronger, your confidence goes up, which is key to getting to your six-figure income goal. Add it to your life plan and you will enjoy it!

Mind Programming

The mind can be programmed just like a computer. It can be programmed to react certain ways, say certain things, and think a certain way. However, just like a computer, it may not <u>always</u> perform its programming the way we would like it to, but we can get pretty close. In fact, your mind is already programmed. You have been doing this your whole life without knowing it. Now, you will learn to program it with purpose, to help you achieve what you need and want. This section is so powerful because it is jam packed with actionable advice that is so simple it can be utilized immediately and impact your life. We are going to mention some things that were referenced in chapter one, like auto suggestion, plus we will go over what physical actions can be taken to program the mind on how we want it to think, talk, and act. The techniques we will delve into will be the power of appearance, speech, and behavior. When simple adjustments are made to how we look, our vocabulary, and how we act and treat others, amazing things happen.

Appearance

Picture this: a person wants to reach a six-figure income and hasn't shaved or fixed their hair all day, their clothes don't fit and are stained, they constantly seem tired, annoyed, and sound depressed and vulgar. How likely is that person to reach their goal any time soon? Most would agree the answer would be not very likely.

Having and maintaining a clean, neat, and—during business activities—professional appearance is a very important part of reaching the six-figure income goal and maximizing the mind body connection. When you appear to be doing well by having a good overall appearance you will be treated better by everyone around you. I'm not talking about being a model on the front of a magazine. What I mean by appearance is simply doing the basics so you don't turn off people that could lead to good opportunities. Some of the basics are bathing regularly, proper body grooming like shaving, having hair cut and styled, make up done correctly, and wearing clean unwrinkled clothing.

One reason this is important to focus on is you never know where your next opportunity is going to come from, so you should always be putting your best foot forward. I can't count how many times I've been in a high level management meeting discussing who to promote and someone would be brought up and one of the managers would say something like, "He cant even shave everyday and you want him to run the department?" Or, "She doesn't even iron her clothes, and you want her to manage others?" That might not sound fair but that is the way a lot of people think. They figure if you can't do the basics to take care of yourself, how can you be handed more responsibility? Other times it's not even consciously realized, meaning a person might not know they don't care for a person because of their appearance, there's just something in their mind is saying 'nope, not them, they rub me the wrong way'. Don't be on the wrong side of that silly judgment; present yourself well, you're worth it.

The second reason, and the reason appearance is in the mind programming section, is the better you look, the better you feel. It is another part of the mind body connection. Everyone has experienced this feeling before. Remember the last time you got a really great haircut? Or bought a dress or suit that fit you perfectly? You probably couldn't stop looking in the mirror. Remember how you felt? You walked a little straighter, had more energy, and were in an overall better mood. Although looks are far from the most important thing in life, that doesn't mean we should neglect them either. Put that extra effort in when you get ready in the morning so you can have all the confidence you need and deserve.

AAA: Make the little things you can do daily to look better a part of your routine. Style your hair, shave, iron your clothes, do your makeup, shine your shoes. Small things like this will make you feel more confident and will open up more opportunities to you. People will look at you and treat you different. So do yourself a favor, take care of your appearance!

Vocabulary

Focusing and making necessary changes to the way you speak is another way to program the mind. Let's introduce what I like to call power vocabulary. Power vocabulary is using words that are positive, upbeat, strong, and truly transformative to the person using them and the person hearing them. For instance if someone asks you, "How are you?" common answers may be, 'I'm ok', 'fine', 'good', and so on. What I want you to do is, no matter your mood, replace those responses with 'excellent, 'fantastic', or 'great'. If someone asks you to do something, instead of replying, 'ok', or 'fine', say 'no problem!', 'done!', or 'you got it!'. Using words like this not only change the conversation you were having but also program your mind to believe the words you are saying, even if you don't! I tell my employees all the time that the only person I lie to is myself. When I'm not feeling well, or I'm stressed out, or tired, I lie to myself. I tell myself I am great! My day was awesome! Fantastic! It's another example of auto suggestion.

For example, I have a routine as soon as I leave work. I call my fiancé and she always asks me "How was your day?" I always reply "excellent!" These responses come out automatically, and my mind follows suit. No matter how my day actually was, all I'm thinking is how great it was. I constantly am programming my mind with positive, powerful vocabulary any chance I get.

AAA: Say these words out loud right now with a little force, like you really mean it: Excellent! Fantastic! Super! Great! Wonderful! No problem! Done! Say them a few times and with conviction. You should feel a little better already. Imagine incorporating these into your speech every day. It is a game changer.

It will transform your relationships, both business and personal, and will keep your mind on the right track, the track we want it on—thinking everything is great! Do you think your mind performs better when it is positive and thinking things are great? Or when it is stressed out and depressed? The answer is obvious, and one way to make sure that your brain is performing at its best and most creative is to use the correct vocabulary in your everyday life.

Another way to take power vocabulary to the next level to program the mind even better is to do the exercise we just spoke about, saying the power words out loud, but do it in the mirror with a huge smile on your face. You might want to make sure no one is around because it may appear a little strange. Despite how silly you may look, it <u>will</u> have an immediate impact on your mood. This is a great exercise to do in the car before an important meeting, like an interview. Between the smiling and the power vocabulary your mind will be so flushed with positivity, it will be forced to be happier! This section is full of actionable advice that may sound a little strange to you but these are proven ways to program your mind to improve mood, be happier, and therefore perform better. Enjoy it!

Behavior

How you act is another important part of the mind body connection. If you are always mean to people, have a scowl on, and are hunched over looking at the ground, your mind will follow. You can tell a lot about a person by how they treat others, especially those below them, like employees or kids. One must treat others with kindness and compassion and patience if that is how one wants to be treated themselves. Like the golden rule says, "Treat others how you would like to be treated."

Just like a bad appearance can thwart a possible opportunity, so can poor behavior. If you are always having outbursts, throwing things in anger, or cursing at people, your name will come up less when opportunities for promotions and such are discussed. Who wants someone who can't control themselves to be in control of a department or company? If your employees are constantly upset or quitting because you speak to them condescendingly, or rudely, it will be difficult to grow that business to its fullest potential.

Perhaps more importantly, how you act is how your mind will act as well. If you behave depressed, or rude, or walk hunched over and never have a smile on your face, your mind will do the same. Conversely, if you treat others well, walk upright with your chest out, and try to smile and laugh whenever you can, your mind will help you do that instead. I remember when I first got into the business world when I was young, people would always say to me, 'smile!' At first I ignored them, but as I began to analyze my behavior to transform myself from kid to businessman, I realized they were right! I never smile! In fact, I was always scowling. I made the change right away and I noticed my first impressions with people changed dramatically, and therefore so did my production, and therefore so did my life! Just by smiling more!

AAA: SMILE!!!

It can be hard to take a unbiased, deep look at yourself and try to change and improve, but it must be done. Are you arrogant? If so, make some changes. Perhaps you have to listen more and talk less. Do you let your temper go out of control? Make it a habit to do some breathing exercises to calm yourself. There are many ways we can all program ourselves to make improvements. What do you need to work on? If you're not sure, ask trusted people and get their opinions. Ask a few though, not just one. When getting opinions about changes you need to make you will want a consensus of a group, not just the opinion of one. However, once you do it and make some changes and see the benefits, it is invigorating. A whole new world of opportunity opens up to you. I once heard "A person's originations have nothing to do with their future." In other words, you can become whoever you like. You only have one life, don't spend it being someone you think you have to be, spend it being who you want to be!

KEY #3

Career Choice

Now that you have a great mindset; a strong, healthy (or maybe getting there) body; and a great appearance, behavior, and vocabulary; you are ready to find the career that will help you get to the six-figure income you desire. Or perhaps with the information you have learned from the previous chapters you can turn your current career into a six-figure earner. With either situation, this chapter is equally important because it will give you some insight on career choices, interviewing strategies, networking, and some skills to help you achieve greatness at whatever career you choose.

Most of us spend the vast majority of our time at our jobs. Especially high earners. Studies show that most six-figure earners work 60-plus hours per week. This is a change that I understand may be hard for some of you reading this book. However, if you are truly dedicated to that six-figure goal, if your <u>why</u> is strong enough, you should have no problem with it. It goes back to mindset and having the correct perspective. If you have the mindset that you will do anything to achieve this goal because your reason, your <u>why</u> is so important to you, a 60-plus hour work week should be no problem. You might even want to push it to 80! Now some more of you may be saying, "Take it easy! 80 hours?." Let me explain. Working more is one of the quickest ways to increase your income, but also is one of the things that make a lot of people cringe. I will show you how working more, as long as it is to accomplish your goals, isn't cringe-worthy at all; actually, it's inspiring!

I remember having a conversation with a dear friend of mine many years ago. He was at a crossroads in his career, working for a family construction business that he enjoyed but there was no pension, and the hours sometimes got long if an emergency popped up or a project had to get finished. If he kept learning he could perhaps open his own company one day where his earnings could be huge. He also had another opportunity arise to work for the government where there was a pension, hours were set at around 40 a week, but there was never going to be any way to earn a lot of money. He asked me my opinion on which he should choose. I told him the choice is simple. What is more important to you—money, or time off? It became clear working as little as possible and having as much time off as he could was more important to him. Shortly thereafter he quit his construction job and started working for the government.

You may be thinking, why didn't I convince him to stick with the construction and open his own business? The reason is that would not have made him happy. His idea of success was weekends and evenings off, taking day trips to the beach, and a lot of vacation time. So the government job was perfect. However, if you're reading this book, chances are those things aren't as important as earning big money. The point I'm making here is if your goal is six-figure income, you have to start thinking bigger. Don't think about not having weekends off, think the weekends are extra time you have to earn more. Don't dwell on not being home for dinner at 5:30 every night, think about what kind of dinners you will have when you can eat wherever and whatever you want.

Dismiss whatever preconceived notions you have about how much you are supposed to work. Just throw them out of your head, and open your mind. Society has programmed us into thinking that 40 hours a week of work is plenty. More than that and you have no life, you need time to do what you want to. It's all crap. Look at the time you have and make your own decision. As was stated in a previous chapter there is 168 hours in a week. If you work 40 hours and sleep 56 hours (that is 8 hours a day, which is a little much), you have 72 hours a week left over. That is almost double the traditional 40-hour work week, to do what? To be clear, I am a family man, and I completely understand the importance of spending quality time with family. If you take the 72 hours and divide it by 7 days in a week that is about 10 hours a day. Do you need to spend 10 hours a day with family to be a good father, mother, brother, sister, son, daughter, or any other duty? Of course not. The point is that working more than 40 hours a week isn't the issue, time management is. If you are going to work 60-plus hour work weeks you better make the off work hours count to have a balanced life.

Studies show that the average person watches 4-5 hours of television a day. I like to veg out in front of the TV from time to time too, but 4-5 hours a day? When it's all over and we look back on our lives, are we going to be happy we spent 30 hours a week staring at a TV? Or are we going to wish we would have done something more meaningful with that time. Perhaps produce more income for ourselves or our families? Or exercise, read, or chase our passions more? That is what I mean when I say you must begin to think bigger. Like we spoke about in our life planning section, we are only given so much time on this earth, let's spend it the best way we can. Learn to limit electronics as a whole, don't lie around in bed for more than you need to, and you will find putting in 60-plus hours a week to achieve your goals is not only doable, it's a pleasure!

Six-Figure Fields

Now that you have opened your eyes and see how much time you really have every week to make big things happen, you should feel a sense of excitement, freedom, and ambition. With a little life planning and time management, you can open up many hours a week to dedicate to achieving your six-figure goal. It's now time to find a career field that will give you the six-figure opportunity you desire. Before we dive into that though, I want to reinforce the importance of the previous chapters. Make sure you understand and put into practice what you read as much as you can because you will need that knowledge and those skills to maximize your opportunity in whatever field you choose.

This section is not going to be a huge list of every single job that can pay six figures. It is however going to educate you on many careers that can pay six figures. Perhaps careers that you would have not considered, or that you didn't really know much about. Also, some of the choices we will go over may shock you as six-figure earners.

Most importantly though, this section will challenge some beliefs you may have about certain jobs, and the way you perceive them.

There is a common misconception that in order to earn six-figures you must be a doctor, a lawyer, or some other career that takes 8-10 years of schooling. Don't believe it! Especially today, there are many different opportunities to get to the six-figure mark without even a basic college education, never mind law or medical school, and you don't necessarily have to work more or harder than those doctors or lawyers. Plus, as a bonus you wont have those huge tuitions to pay for!

If someone were to ask me what the number one field to go into to make six-figures is, I would tell them sales without hesitation. The first reason being most sales jobs have no limit on income. The amount you make is directly related to your production. So many employees today feel that they are not rewarded properly for their efforts. That doesn't happen in a sales position. When the salesperson sells more product, the company makes more money, and therefore the salesperson gets rewarded financially. That is how it should work! It's a beautiful thing!

The second reason is learning how to sell could quite possibly be the most important trait that a high earning hopeful needs to have. Everything needs to be sold. Think about it. Look around the room you are in right now. Think about the products you use every day. They were all sold. Your furniture, clothing, cars, house, telephones, computers, the list goes on and on. These products are all sold in different ways, but they are all sold. Some depend on actual salespeople being face to face with the customer, some rely heavily on marketing, but they all need to be sold. Therefore, learning as much as you can about sales is the single best tool to have in your six-figure tool belt.

For some, the word 'sales' has a bad connotation of pushy, sleazy, greedy salespeople. Like any group of people there is going to be the good, the bad, and the ugly. Sales is no different. You could say the same for the previously mentioned lawyers and doctors. When I say I want you to learn how to sell, I mean how to communicate properly, demonstrate a product effectively, and close. That is the essence of being a salesperson. When someone learns to become a salesperson their life changes forever. When you learn to impose your will effectively, convincingly, and professionally, there is no limit to what you can accomplish, both in the business world and in your personal life. Don't forget, it's not just products that need to be sold. Boyfriends or girlfriends need to be sold on the idea of marrying you, children have to be sold on the idea of doing their homework, and so on. Show me a successful person and I'll show you that they are a good salesperson. A lawyer needs to sell the jury on the fact their client is innocent. A doctor has to sell the patient on the fact that they will heal them. A business owner needs to sell his product. A high level union worker has to sell his superiors that he is worthy of the promotions that got him there. Even if your job is not labeled as a salesperson, everyone needs to learn to sell. For now, let's go back to those positions that are labeled as salespeople.

There are many different sales positions that can yield a six-figure income with no experience or formal education. Some may require brief training to be able to do the job, but those trainings are minimal and usually free of charge. Some examples of these positions would be real estate agent, insurance sales, car sales, furniture sales, cable TV rep, boat sales, clothing sales, and many different business to business sales like software, copiers, etc. To be clear, to earn six figures in any of these types of positions you have to be a top performer, or else everyone would do it! Almost anyone can be a top performer in a position like this; it's not easy, but nothing worthwhile ever is. It takes determination, hard work, focus, and once again a strong why. You will need that strong why because you will experience a lot of rejection and self doubt, but you must push through those and keep going, knowing it will be worth it. One of the best feelings in life is knowing you can always produce a good living. If you become an expert salesperson you will feel just that. Top salespeople are, and always will be, in demand anywhere there are businesses that need to sell their product. In a later chapter we will go into educating and training yourself to transform into a professional, and very valuable sales person, but for now let's talk about some other six-figure job options.

Another great career path to take to six figures is management. Companies are always looking for great managers to help run their business the way they want. Competent, hardworking, and ambitious managers are key to the everyday success of any company. They instill the correct processes, policies, and help push production and therefore profit. Since they are so important they are often handsomely rewarded with large salaries and bonuses. A lot of large companies even have management training programs where you start as an assistant manager and you can work your way up. Some examples of companies where you can work your way up to the six-figure positions are Wal-Mart, Home Depot, Lowe's, and most large companies like those. However, like most things that pay off, these positions are not easy. They usually demand a lot of hours and can come with a lot of pressure to make sure your department or store is running properly. It's not just large companies that generously reward great managers, a lot of smaller companies pay a lot of money for someone they can count on to get the job done. Companies like this that come to mind are construction companies, car dealerships, and large restaurants.

There are many blue collar ways to six figures as well. If you like to work with your hands more that is perfectly fine. As a matter of fact, that is great! America was built on the backs of hard working blue collar people. I have known many iron workers, electricians, contractors, and mechanics that make six figures. To earn money like this these people are obviously at the top of their field, just like the salespeople previously mentioned. Their work barely even needs to be checked by superiors because they take pride in doing things correctly, and most importantly efficiently to get as much done as possible.

In these types of positions the key to the big paychecks is sometimes overtime, especially if it's a union job. It is possible to earn time and a half or double time, then the money really adds up. Also some of these positions' pay structure is based off of 'book time'. For example, an auto mechanic needs to replace a transmission. The 'book' may say it requires three hours of labor. If the mechanic does it in two hours, they still get paid for the book time of three hours. Then in that third hour they can start a new job while still getting paid another hour for the previous one. Now they are earning double! See, in almost any field there is a way to get big paychecks, you simply must be looking for it.

Opening your mind and changing your way of thinking towards which career fields can really pay off. Some people would never think of selling cars or furniture, but then when they think about making $100k-plus by doing so, many reconsider. Then if you master that and work your way up to run your own dealership or store you are looking at $250k a year plus! With no degree! Just some determination, goals, hard work, and a strong why. This world is absolutely packed with opportunity to earn big, you just have to open your eyes and go get it.

Show Up

Are you having actionable advice withdrawal? This is some of the best actionable advice in this entire book, so it gets its own section.

AAA: SHOW UP! Yup, that's it. So much more in life can get accomplished by simply showing up. If you say to yourself or to someone else that you are going to be somewhere at a certain time, do it! Show up!

So many people make a commitment and never even show up. So many opportunities are blown like this. The saddest part is the majority of people most likely don't even realize it because they convinced themselves that the best thing to do is not to go. This section refers to showing up primarily in regards to employment, but for a moment let's talk about other situations where showing up is important in everyday life.

Many single people looking for a relationship meet someone that they are attracted to or connect with and make plans to go on a date. A couple days go by and the day comes, and they get cold feet. They start to rationalize why they can't go. They are too busy, too tired, a friend said that person is not their type, and they back out. They don't show up to what could have been someone that could change their life. Or they force themselves to go, they show up, and fall head over heels in love and get married, and have a fantastic life together. That person will always remember what showing up when they were scared to awarded them. You have to show up! What is the worst that could happen? You cut the date short and wasted a couple hours. What is the best that could happen? You could meet the love of your life!

How many people make plans to go to work out and never show up? They go to the gym, meet with the salesperson, take a tour of the facility, and go home with all the excitement in the world. This is it! I'm going to get in shape! Then the next day they get out of work, gym bag in the car, and begin to rationalize why they shouldn't go. They are tired from a long day at work, don't feel well, it's raining, and they drive right past the gym. If you make that promise to yourself you must keep it. You must show up! Pull into the gym, get out, go in, and work out. It is a guarantee you will feel so much better after that workout then if you just went home and watched TV. Then you show up the next day, and the day after that, and before you know it going to the gym is not just something you do, it's a part of your life. When it becomes a part of your life, you will be healthier, have more energy, and live longer, just by showing up!

Think of situations you have been in where you didn't show up, or perhaps you almost didn't, and you forced yourself to go and great things happened.

Showing up in your career carries the same, if not more importance. Whether it's showing up for an interview, a meeting, or just to work every day, you must show up. The words 'show up' are going to appear a lot in this section, so let's dive a little deeper into what I mean by 'show up'.

The first part of showing up is preparation. You must be ready before you even get there. A good night's sleep is the first step to being prepared. Without enough rest your mind won't be as sharp as you need it to be to handle situations, make decisions, and speak properly. You can't be out partying all night, get two hours of sleep and expect to perform your best. The next part of being prepared is being dressed properly and neatly. This goes back to the appearance section in an earlier chapter. Make sure your clothes are ironed and being worn correctly. You can't be in the company's lobby tying your tie or putting makeup on and expect be viewed as a six-figure earner.

The next part of showing up is punctuality. Be on time! If you are supposed to be somewhere at 8am, make sure you are there by 7:45am. For some this comes naturally, for others it is almost impossible. I can't count how many people I have seen lose a job opportunity or get fired because they can't be on time. It is always something with these types of people, and maybe you are one of them. They have a flat tire, traffic was bad, car wouldn't start, etc. That is why you must make it a habit to be early, then if something unexpected does happen, you are still okay. If you master punctuality, you are putting yourself way ahead of most as it is so hard for many people to accomplish this seemingly simple task. Perhaps it is because of all the distractions we have in our lives today, but it is a major issue with today's work force. What worse way to start an interview than being late? Who is going to get promoted, or given more responsibility, or a raise? The person who is always late? Or the person who is always 15 minutes early? So get up, get moving, and be on time!

The final part of showing up is honoring your commitments. If you commit to doing something, make sure you do it. If you made the appointment, whatever it is, you did it for a reason. Maybe it was an interview for a better job, a meeting with a client to demonstrate a new product, or a task you have been putting off. You committed to it because you know it needs to be done, but then fear, procrastination, and laziness begin to rear their ugly heads, and you start to talk yourself out of it. You must realize when this is happening and fight it. Mastering this will bring you further than you can imagine. You will develop a reputation of being reliable, and consistent, which in the business world is huge. How many times have you worked with a company that doesn't show up when they say they are going to, or doesn't get documents to you when they said they would? It probably drives you crazy, right? Even if it's something as simple as the plumber for your house. He says he'll be there at 2pm and gets there by 3:15pm without calling to let you know. It shows a lack of respect for your patronage and your time. Don't be that person! Be the person that shows up when they say they will, on time and prepared!

Interview

In the search for your future six-figure career you will inevitably be going on some job interviews. For many the words 'job interview' bring up feelings of worry, fear, sleepless nights, and so on. This section is going to give you some simple, actionable tips to give you the confidence you need so you will not feel so stressed. This section will also go over what employers look for in an interview, both good and bad, so you will know what to do and what not to do to absolutely crush your next interview!

AAA: The day before your interview you must make sure you have copies of your resume printed and ready to go. The last thing you want is to go to print your resume the morning of the interview and run out of ink or paper. Have your outfit picked out the night before. To ensure you will arrive on time to the interview, which is absolutely vital, make sure you plan out your route the day before and leave plenty of time for traffic. In some highly competitive fields being late could disqualify you before you even get started. I stress doing as much as possible the night before because the focus the day of the interview shouldn't be on simple things like directions and clothing. It should be on performing and putting your best foot forward.

Your clothing should of course be fitting for the industry you are interviewing in. Most indoor professional jobs require men to wear a suit and tie, and women to wear a business suit either with pants or a skirt that reaches the knees. Suits should be gray, black, or blue, as those are considered business suits. Shirts should be light in color as this exudes cleanliness and professionalism. Small things like this really matter as the clothing you wear is a big part of the first impression and also makes an impression on the employer's subconscious. Keep jewelry to a minimum, and make sure shoes are shined. Men should of course be clean shaven and women should do their makeup in a professional business-like manner. Even if you are not going for an office position, over-dressing will never hurt, but under-dressing certainly will.

If possible, make sure you silence your phone. Along with copies of your resume bring two pens in case one chooses not to work. You don't want to have to write something down and not have a pen. That suggests lack of preparedness, which is not a good trait to show to an employer!

Now, you look good, smell good, and you're on time. The interviewer approaches you and you give a firm hand shake, a big smile, and good eye contact. Those three behaviors are simple ways to get things off on the right foot. Next, you sit down in an office. It is said that 80% of communication is non-verbal. That 80% is made up of body language like your posture, facial expressions, and hand movements. I could write forever on body language but that is not the goal here. However, I will give you some tips. Make sure you sit up straight with good posture. Being hunched over exudes old age and poor health. Do not fidget with your fingers or shake your feet. This shows nervousness and can be distracting. Feel free to use your hands to express yourself and to get a point across but don't overdo it. Do not touch your hands to your mouth or rest your chin on your hands as this conveys fatigue and possibly boredom. Your hands should be folded in your lap or whatever is comfortable, once again, without being distracting.

You're in there giving it your best. Be prepared to answer tough interview questions. Some examples of these are, "What is your biggest strength?" "What is your biggest weakness?" "Why should you be chosen for this position?" There are many of these difficult questions interviewers may ask. They are designed to throw you off a little bit, to see how you think on the fly and get a better feel for you and what you're about. Be prepared for queries like these, it could come in handy.

When an employer is looking to hire someone, they are searching for an employee who is going to help take the company to the next level. Someone that will give them an edge, a unique experience, perhaps knowledge that can push the company forward. What is special about you that will do this for them? That is what you will want to showcase. Do you have certain skills from a previous job? Special training? Maybe you can outwork anyone, or you can work anytime. Prove these skills with any accomplishments you have achieved, like awards, bonuses you've received, or titles you have held. A great way to stand out is showing how you will make the interviewer themselves more successful, or how you will make their job easier.

You will want to seem confident but not cocky. Confidence shows you are the real deal. Being cocky shows you are overcompensating for a lack of confidence. The latter will turn an employer off almost immediately. It is a good idea to have some questions prepared that you want to ask. Have them written down so you don't forget them in the pressure of the interview. Asking these questions of course gives you answers to things you want to know about the position or the company, but it also shows attentiveness and interest.

When it seems the interview is coming to an end and you want the position don't be afraid to ask for it. This shows ambition and courage. An example of the wording you may want to use is, "All that being said do you feel comfortable offering me the position?" They may hire you on the spot or they may have other interviews they must do, but asking for it will tell them you really want it and will work hard if you get it.

Lastly, be yourself. Be the best version of yourself, but be yourself. The reason I stress this is there is no point to giving off an impression you are person "A" when in reality you are person "D". In other words, you don't want to pretend to be someone you are not because sooner or later you will drop that facade and your position there could end because of it. An integral part of having success and longevity at a job is fitting in. If you get the distinct impression that is not going to happen, you may want to keep looking. I am not telling you to be picky, because if you are trying to get your foot in the door you will probably have to put up with a lot, all I'm saying is let your personality shine through and you will do great!

Networking

A huge part of your long term success in your chosen career is networking. I've found that this topic means different things to different people. What I am going to speak about in relation to networking is simply having many connections in your field so you will <u>always</u> have a job, and so opportunities will always be opening up to you. There is an old saying, "It's not what you know, it's who you know." This section will show you how to never have to look in advertisements for a job, and if you need one you will reach out to your network, not the help wanted section. This is extremely important as I will get you to the point where your company is lucky to have you, not the other way around. Many people today live in constant fear of losing their job, but that is not necessary, and once you do not have that worry about anymore you will be more productive, happier, and more free than ever!

The type of networking discussed in this section is what I call organic networking. Organic networking is about building up your value, your own personal brand if you will. It is not about using different tactics to network with thousands of people, or about packing your social media with thousands of contacts. It is about having a reputation that is earned the old fashioned way. First, by being an expert in your field. Second, with a great work ethic. Lastly, by treating people right.

Being an Expert

Being an expert in your field is very important when it comes to networking. No one is going to recommend you for a position of any significance if you do not know what you are doing. If they did, then their reputation would plummet when you didn't perform in the position they helped you get. The idea of becoming an expert in your industry is simple. You learn as much as possible about it and execute what you learn. The nice thing about this is, being so knowledgeable will make you a high performer, which should be very rewarding in itself, with the side benefit of building a great reputation that will help with your networking.

This all begs the question, "How do I become an expert?" To truly become and expert means to know more than the majority of your peers. How much does the average employee learn about their job, field, or business? Usually just as much as they need to get by. By going the extra mile in learning your craft, you will become an expert. Some examples are going to seminars, reading books, learning hands on from more experienced people in your field, etc. This is the information age. If you want to learn, you can, no doubt about it. You have to be like a sponge soaking up the knowledge wherever you can.

If you're a salesman, you could learn about psychology. What makes a person buy? You could learn new closes or selling strategies. A good salesman knows their product right? Go to seminars provided by your manufacturer and read the manuals. If you're a science teacher, go on whale watching trips, or visit an observatory. Or perhaps go to conferences about different, more effective ways to teach and for your students to learn. If you're an office manager you could learn about new software that organizes the company's finances better, or learn about management to lead the other office personnel more effectively to get more accomplished.

There are countless ways to get the knowledge to reach the top of your field. The point I'm trying to make here is there is room to improve and become an expert in any career. You just have to look for it. Once you do people will start looking up to you. They will begin to ask your for advice or opinion. Then guess who will be considered for the next promotion? Or when someone you worked with leaves the company for another and they have a better position there that needs to be filled, who is that person going to recommend? YOU! The expert, of course.

Have a Great Work Ethic

You have probably heard it all your life. Work ethic, work ethic, work ethic. But what does it really mean? How can you be viewed as having it? Do you have it? Well, let's take a look.

The definition of 'ethic' is "a set of moral principles." So work ethic is a set of moral principles about work. First, start with punctuality. No one is going to be thought of as a great worker if they are never on time. Earlier we spoke more about this so I won't go too far into it again, but be on time! Secondly, you have to get the job done. Supervisors, managers, bosses, and even peers like to know they can count on you to get the job done. They want to know that when they hand you that assignment they don't have to constantly check up on it to see if it's getting done. So be the person that <u>always</u> finishes the task at hand no matter what, on time and correctly. Lastly, and this is probably the least popular one. . . work a lot. Good old fashion overtime, burning the midnight oil, whatever you want to call it. Learn to love working a lot. Instead of thinking, "Ugh, I have to work this weekend," think "Yes! I get overtime this weekend!" So many people can't even find a job and I have more work than I need! Think about the extra money you will earn and what you could do with it. Most importantly think about the service you are doing your superior and your company, and although that might not have an immediate effect, it will certainly have a long term one. You will be the one the department can 'count on'. That will do wonders for your reputation and therefore your network.

Besides the money, and the respect you get from having a great work ethic, there is something else that comes along with it too. We all know that feeling you get after a long day's work, or completing a big project, or hitting a big sales goal. It's called self satisfaction, and it feels great. Like when you were a kid and you cleaned up your messy room. You sit back and soak it up and think, "I did that." You feel on top of the world, proud, and accomplished. Learn to love that feeling and you will chase it. Then you're not just doing it for the financial reward, or to look good, you're doing it to feel good, and sometimes that is the best motivator of all.

Treat People Right

Have you ever heard someone say, "I know who would be perfect for that position, and they are a real jerk"? I doubt it. People like to help and recommend people they like, and if you are rude, condescending, unfriendly, or deceitful, people aren't going to like you. So lets go through some not so obvious ways this can be accomplished.

AAA: Treat everyone the same, from the bottom of the totem pole to the top.

Most successful people will tell you they treat everyone in their company the same, from the janitor all the way up to the CEO. This is a vital behavior that must be learned and used because it shows that you are a kind and respectful person, period. Not just to those above you to make a good impression, but to everyone. This one behavior will bring you tremendous respect and loyalty from your co-workers. Both those in positions above and below yours. Have you ever seen someone treat a person they are in charge of poorly just because they can? It is awful and it makes the underling feel awful. If you do that to someone, or in front of someone, most people will never forget it. The reason why some people behave that way is because of their own insecurities. It makes them feel better to put down someone else because they aren't happy with who they are for one reason or another. So if you are one of these people, find your insecurities, and learn to overcome them so you can treat people with the dignity they deserve as fellow human beings.

Some examples of this would be to say hi to the maintenance man instead of just walking by him. Or wave to the landscapers when they are working in 95 degree heat. Or make sure to thank the mail room clerk when they bring you your mail. We know how to do it but many of us don't. Sometimes you may behave poorly toward people below you for malicious reasons, or sometimes your mind was just somewhere else. Whatever the reason, make it a point to follow the golden rule at work and everywhere else. Treat others as you would like to be treated. Maybe even better!

KEY #4

Education

On to the next key on your way to a six-figure income: education. This is the 4th key by design. Knowing what the correct mindset is, understanding your mind body connection, and contemplating or perhaps acting on the correct career choice is important before choosing your next step in your education.

What we are going to talk about may not be what you think of when you hear the word education. I am going to talk to you about an education that will earn you not just money, but also respect, self-esteem, confidence, and the ability to help others more. It is sad that the vast majority of people stop their education after high school or college. I'm sure you have heard something similar to this before, but education should never stop. There is so much out there to learn to make you not only a better earner, but also a better husband or wife, employee, manager, and overall human being. Unfortunately, or fortunately, if these people are your competition, most only educate themselves when it is necessary for a job or an event of some sort. Your brain is built to absorb knowledge and facts, and accomplish amazing things. However, if we don't use it, and continually push it to work, it is like a muscle, it will get weak and its performance will decline. It will begin to act sluggish and groggy. The worst part is, this decline is so gradual you may not even notice it happening. If you are reading this book you obviously don't want this to happen to you. You want your brain to be sharp and alert and kicking out great thoughts and ideas all the time. So use that muscle in between your ears! Make it work, and it will get strong and help you accomplish truly amazing things!

I know some of you reading this may be thinking, "Ugh... education, I hated school!" Don't worry, I hated school too, but I love to learn, and so will you. The reason you will like the education we will speak about is it has an immediate, direct impact on your life. We wont be discussing history from 400 years ago, or calculus problems, or anything else that has almost no part in your daily life. We will be discussing an education that will help you the very moment you learn it. You need to learn things targeted to helping you in whatever areas you want to improve in, that will have a positive impact on your life right away. Not only will your life improve dramatically with the correct education, but the results you get will make you want to continue , creating a snowball effect of learning and knowledge.

To be clear, I am not hating on traditional methods of education, like college. There are schools of higher learning all over the world that have fantastic curriculum and undoubtedly mean well. If you are reading this and have a college degree, congratulations. I know it takes a lot of hard work and dedication to graduate, but most don't teach you a thing about how to financially prosper in today's world and that is what we are talking about. By the time I was 22 I had many college graduates both young and old working for me, a guy who never went to or even had a desire to go to college.

I remember when I was 19 at my first sales job, I was working beside college graduates in the same position I was in except they had $75,000 in student loans. I'll never forget that, it had a big impact on me. I would ask them, "Why did you go to college?" I got many different answers but they all had the same message. It was simply what you do after high school. The truth of the matter is college has turned into a business, plain and simple. Sadly, it now starts many recent graduates in their adult lives with tons of debt and sometimes even sadder, a degree that does nothing for them in the real world.

If you went to college, or some other form of higher learning great, let's build on that education. If not, no worries, you can start your education now!

Types of Education

Let's now speak about some options you have when it comes to your education. There are so many avenues in today's world to gain knowledge within. This section will go over some of the options I've used throughout the years to help me achieve many wonderful things, go places I never thought I would, help more people than I thought possible, and live better than anyone I know.

BOOKS

Possibly the oldest, most utilized, tried and true method of learning is reading books. "Those who read, lead"! That is another one of my mantras I live by. Why do those who read lead? The answer is simple. As a result of their reading they know more than most other people, therefore they lead them. When you read a lot you also increase your vocabulary which makes you a better speaker and communicator. It is said that the average CEO reads 50 books a year. Think about that! That is almost a book a week! Think about all the knowledge and expertise that comes along with that much reading. No wonder these CEO's make such huge salaries and have so much impact on their companies and beyond.

You are reading this book, so you must understand that reading and learning through books is important. I applaud you because you are the minority. I do however want to further explain why books are so important to learning and success. There are the obvious reasons: Books teach you how to do things you didn't previously know how to do. They open up your mind to think in ways you didn't previously think. You can obtain different perspectives on nearly everything. Other cultures, both ancient and modern day, can be explored, opening your eyes like never before. Motivations can be discovered, pushing you forward with confidence obtained by reading other people's stories and taking their lead.

Then there is the less obvious yet very simple reason why books are so vital to living the best life possible. Reading **HOW** to do something and getting it right the first time will propel your progress forward by leaps and bounds, compared to learning it on your own and accomplishing it by trial and error, or perhaps not at all. This benefit mostly applies to non-fiction. The person writing the book is (or at least should be, do your research) an expert on whatever they are writing about. They know how to do it and are sharing the knowledge with you, the reader, so you don't have to make the same or perhaps more mistakes than they did. How great is that? They take the bumps and bruises, the let downs, the failures, and teach you how to avoid them and succeed. What a deal!

Another great benefit to this type of learning is you have a tangible hard copy of what you learned. So you can go back and reference it anytime you want. I have books on my shelf I have read multiple times, every time picking up something new, and remembering something I have let slip out of my mind. A situation may arise and I'll think to myself, I'm not positive on the best way to handle that, let me go back to the book I read on that topic and see what it says again. The problem that pops up could be anything from a business issue, to a relationship problem, to a quote you want to remember.

Audio books are great too. If you can absorb information well by listening it can be a great way to spend a commute to work or any other long drive. Personally, I prefer to read the physical copy first.

Then perhaps years later if I want to read and book over again I get the audio version and listen to it in the car, to re-visit all the great content without taking up any reading time dedicated to new books. Everyone takes in information differently so do what is best for you. Some say they don't like to read, or they aren't a good reader. I urge these people to force themselves to read.

AAA: If you're not a big reader, set a reading quota for yourself. Something like a book a month, or a page quota like 5 or 10 pages a day. Write it down and stick to it. You will be amazed how many books you can read when you read a little every day. Like anything else practice makes perfect. Your brain will quickly adapt to the reading again like when you were in school and before long you will be flying through the pages.

Seminars

Going to seminars, or lectures, or conferences, whatever the label, is also a great source of education. It is even better when you see an author that you like in person. Reading what they write is one thing, but seeing and hearing them talk about it, in their own voice with their own emotions, hits you in an entirely different way. The connection you get when you are face to face with these super successful, motivated individuals can be life changing.

I'll tell a quick story that happened in my own life to illustrate this point. It was my first year in sales, I was 19 years old. A representative of someone who is now an icon in the self-help world came to one of our sales meetings. He was selling tickets to the upcoming seminar for around $600, and the company I worked for would pay half. Now please remember I am 19 years old, completely on my own, and not doing so well in my sales career yet. I said $300 to hear some guy speak? I'll pass!

Well a bunch of the guys I worked with went. They came back under some sort of spell! It was like they were hypnotized! I asked them how it was and they couldn't stop talking about it. These guys thought they had the best job in the world! To be honest I kind of kicked myself. I started doing some research on the guy they went to see speak. I started buying his CDs and reading his books. I absorbed everything he had like a sponge and my career took off! Next year when those reps came around selling tickets I was first in line. I still remember seeing Grant Cardone speak for the first time in person. It was absolutely incredible. He was a force of nature that couldn't be stopped. Back then he just did sales training. Now he does a lot more than that, but wow, I was amazed.

I didn't know there was a **way** to properly sell. I was told the basics on how to do my job, given a desk, and a "good luck!" My career was okay before I started training myself, but once I learned **how** to sell, my income doubled, then the next year doubled again. It was incredible. By the time I was 20 I had my first 5-figure month. I thought I was rich! I learned the best investment in the world is yourself. I know how it is. When that rep asked me for $300 for that seminar that was a lot of money to me. I came to find out that $300 would have made me $3000 in a month or two, never mind in a lifetime! Where else are you going to get that type of return? That is the power of education.

AAA: ABL. Always be learning. Be a sponge, soak it all up! Anywhere you can get knowledge or wisdom, take it. Don't be narrow minded and stubborn like I was.

There are different types of seminars out there. There are short one- to two-hour talks. Then there are self-help seminars that last 5-8 hours. There are also the boot camp types that can last days. They are all great in their own way. Just like reading a book they will give you new ideas, ways of thinking, perspectives—and I think they dish out motivation even better than a book. That in person energy and the passion you get from the crowd is unparalleled in any other type of education.

Mentors

Learning from a mentor is a fantastic source of education. Getting the inside scoop from someone who has done it, and done it well, is a surefire way to propel your education forward immensely. Mentors can come from anywhere. They could be a friend, family member, co-worker, or your boss. As you look for a mentor you must make sure they are qualified to be a mentor. Too many under performers are eager to 'teach', to pass down their 'knowledge', but unbeknownst to them they are simply teaching and passing down ways to also become an under performer. A mentor that you want will be a proven top performer in whatever you are trying to learn. Some examples would be a doctor with a successful practice, a salesperson that holds records for volume or commissions, a mechanic that can fix anything, etc.

I remember my first mentor. He was the second sales manager I had in my career. This man told me when he became my boss that if I listen to him I will be making x amount of dollars. I forget what the exact amount was, but I remember when I noticed he was right. There is nothing like that hands on face to face teaching a mentor can give you. I would run into a problem and he would say to do this and that, and it would work! Then the next time I had that issue, guess what? I knew what to do and could implement it immediately. I was always very grateful for that man, and you will be also if you are lucky to find such a great mentor.

AAA: Find a mentor!!!

Have you ever heard the saying, "A closed mouth never gets fed"? That is true with finding a great mentor. In other words you have to be looking to learn in order for someone to teach you. If you have the attitude that so many have that "I know what I'm doing," you will never find that mentor you need, because who would want to help someone like that? Who would want to take time out of their day and spend their energy on a know it all? You must be eager, ready to learn, and most importantly, ready to change. That last one is the toughest one. People hate change, but in order to get better, change is a must. After all, if you keep doing everything the same way, you will never get different results.

There are all different type of mentors, because there are all different fields to get mentored in. Sometimes you will have to provide value to the person in order for them to mentor you. One hand washes the other. In the case of my first mentor, I was his salesperson, so the value I brought him was selling his product. Therefore, the better salesperson he made me, the more product I sold and money I made the company, hence, the better he did as the manager. It was a true symbiotic relationship. One might think every manager would do that if it helped his department do better. The sad truth is that is not the case. The average sales manager sits back at his desk and waits for the business to come to him. Only the great ones train and can turn an average person, into a great salesperson.

It works in all different types of situations. I realize you may be reading this book thinking you don't want a mentor in sales, so now what? For instance, let's say you want a mentor in real estate investing, and you know someone who is very successful at it. Perhaps you could approach that person and say that you are looking to learn the business, but have no experience; what can you do for them to assist in any way so you could learn? There are a million things you could do. Maybe one of their properties just got renovated. The mentor could walk you through the house and show you what was done to rehab it, and in turn you could clean the inside. Or you could stuff envelopes for all the mail the investor sends out to property owners looking to buy their property, and in turn you could learn about direct mail campaigns and the marketing that goes into it.

You have a ton of value you could add to someone's business in return for some knowledge. Be willing to learn, to do things that you may believe are under you. Start at the bottom, be humble, and you can find a mentor. Then someday you could be someone's mentor. Wouldn't that be great!

KEY #5

Entrepreneurship

The fifth key is entrepreneurship. It is something that most people dream of. Being their own boss. Running **their** business **their** way. Working their own hours and answer to no one but themselves. Sounds great, right? Well it is, or at least it can be. History is filled with great stories of people who started a business from nothing and had tremendous success. However, history is filled with many more stories that are less often heard. Stories of people sinking all their money, time, and health into a business only for it to fail. Why do some businesses thrive and some die? Should I be an entrepreneur? What business would I start? Should I quit my job to do it? How would I start a business? We will discuss these questions and more in this section.

Should I be an Entrepreneur?

Absolutely! Becoming an entrepreneur is a great step to get you to a six-figure income. One of the great things about it is there are so many different ways to become one. Creating income all on your own on your own terms is a fantastic feeling. It is surreal at first because if you have always been an employee, all you know is going to work and getting a paycheck. When you first create your own paycheck it is so much more rewarding. Plus it gives you a feeling of pride and freedom like nothing else! Once you get your first income from your own business there is no limit to what you can accomplish!

One great thing about becoming an entrepreneur is you can start as small as you'd like. You don't have to invest a ton of money or time if you don't have it or don't want to. I know people, including myself, who have started successful businesses in their spare time when they are not working at their job. Some great examples I've seen have been catering, home repair, flipping houses, acquiring rental properties, on-line business, sewing, child care and many more. The ideas and possibilities are endless.

You must look for opportunities. For example, consider the town where you live. What is missing? What does the community need? Maybe there are no good taxis, bagel stores, coffee shops, house cleaning companies, bakeries, bike stores, affordable rental homes, and so on. Find what you could create to serve your community and go for it.

What are you good at? Do you have a special talent that people would pay for? Can you play an instrument, train dogs, make clothing, paint? Or maybe you can sing and dance! I know I'm all over the place here but it is because I am trying to stimulate your thinking. Too often people are stuck in the everyday rut and are unable to see an opportunity staring them in the face. Then they see someone else do it and they say, "I could have done that!"

So we have learned to be on a constant lookout for opportunities. That is great. However, just spotting the opportunity isn't going to do anything without action. Too many people have so many great ideas and do nothing about it. Don't let this be you! I know this is easier said than done, so let me give you a tip. Say you have discovered an opportunity to serve that you think you can build a profitable business around. That's great, but this is where many get stuck. Most people start thinking about what could go wrong or why they can't do it. What if I run out of money? I don't have time. Could I pull it off? Who would work for me? What if? What if?

It is normal to have concerns, and healthy for that matter. Going into business like a bull in a china shop isn't the best idea either. However, don't get stuck in analysis paralysis.

AAA: Everyday take one step toward opening the business, whatever it is. Just one step a day. This will slowly build your confidence and give you the feeling of progress, and eventually end with a business!

For example, if you wanted to start a house cleaning company, perhaps the first day you could see what competitors charge. Then the next day you could price out cleaning supplies. On day three maybe see what maids get paid to clean a house. See, everyday take a small step, make progress. This way you don't get overwhelmed by the thought of it all. It's just one small, relatively easy task a day. You can do that!

Why do some businesses thrive and some die?

There are obviously many answers to this question, and it would be impossible to list them all. We will however go over some of the main reasons why some companies do well and others struggle so that you may have the knowledge to avoid some of these pitfalls and learn from their successes. I have had the privilege to own and run my own successful business and it is a wonderful thing. I hope to give you some tools to help you do the same.

Cost Analysis

One of the big reasons why businesses fail is what I will call incorrect cost analyzing, meaning not estimating expenses accurately. This one is so huge and I see it kill all types of businesses all the time. If you're not aware of it will sneak up on you and crush you. I'll give an example. Have you ever looked at a car wash and seen cars just pouring through it, or a convenience store with people constantly walking in and out of it with goods and thought, that place is a cash cow! Yeah, it may be, or it may lose money every year. How is that possible? There is almost non-stop business. It's possible because of inaccurate cost calculating. Sure, money may be pouring into the business, but if more is pouring out, guess what? It loses money and fails. Some of the main profit killers that the first time entrepreneur might not think of is the rent or mortgage, insurance, fuel, cleaning, payroll, electricity, heat, cooling, weather, signage, advertising, etc. The novice business owner sees a gas station that takes in $35000 dollars a month just in fuel sales and thinks "I'm going to be rich!" Sure, that sounds great. What will the fuel cost you? "That car wash washes 200 cars a day, I'm buying it!" But what about the water bill? How much is the equipment if it needs to be replaced?

What can you do to make sure this doesn't happen to you? Do your research. If you're buying an existing business, get documents from the seller displaying all the costs involved with the business. Anyone who calls themselves a business owner will have some type of accounting system showing income and expenses. Get it and go through it, and ask questions if you are unsure about something. It is better to miss a good deal by being too careful than to buy a bad one by being reckless. If you are starting a new business from the ground up, you won't have paperwork showing all your costs, so you will have to get your information in a different way. Get a piece of paper and start building your own income and expenses sheet. Will you need employees? If yes, how many? What will payroll be? Rent or mortgage cost? Ask the owner of the building you plan to rent what the utilities usually cost. Do they have receipts of that? Are you selling a product? What is the costs of it? Is it a seasonal business? How will you handle the down times?

Those are just a few things you must ask yourself. Ask anyone you know in a similar business what other costs you're missing. Go online and search costs associated with owning that type of business. Are there similar business like the one you want to open nearby? Go patronize it. Sit there a while and watch the business and look for other costs involved.

Systems, Systems, Systems

The most successful businesses in the world have great systems. First let's define what I mean by systems. A system is a step by step process to complete a certain task. The reason why systematizing your business is so important is that the business can continue to operate with the change of personnel. Therefore your business doesn't have to rely on a specific person or people. It can rely on any person because they just have to follow the systems put in place and business continues.

I'll give you an example of what I'm taking about. If I ask a crowd of 100 people, "Who here can make a better cheeseburger than McDonald's?," how many would raise their hands? Probably 90 or more. If 90% of people can make a better burger than McDonald's, then why have they sold more burgers than anybody ever? Why do they continue after all these years to be wildly successful? One word: systems. The systems at McDonald's are so good you can get almost the same burger in almost the same amount of time anywhere in the world where there is a McDonald's. From the moment someone is hired they know exactly what their job is and the steps to take to get it done. This many fries go into the oil for this much time and then they are removed. This much mustard and this much ketchup goes on every burger, etc.

When you go into a McDonald's they are most likely pretty busy, but does anyone look panicked, running around, not knowing what they are doing? Not that I have ever seen. Everyone has their head down doing their job over, and over, and over again. When someone leaves do people no longer get their burger or their fries in a few minutes? Nope. Someone else is hired, taught the system they are responsible for, and business moves right along. It's a beautiful thing.

However, when a first time entrepreneur opens their business, do they have written systems in place for every position in the company? Not likely. Most of the time the owner attempts to do everything themselves. Thinking, "No one can do it better than me so why would I have someone else do it?" Then before long they burn out. They are wearing too many hats and it drives them nuts. Who is going to do all this when this person gets sick? Business shuts down? Customers aren't serviced? What about vacation? Those don't exist anymore?

Or they do hire employees but fail to give them the systems they need to do their job properly so they do it their way, which isn't quite right but it's okay. Then another employee, and another, all doing it <u>their</u> way, instead of the <u>right</u> way. What happens when one of those employees leaves? Another one is hired and that person has to learn how to do the job, and they do it <u>their</u> way. This results in inconsistent customer service and products. Have you ever been to a restaurant and the food was great, but the next time you went it wasn't as good? Have you ever gotten your car serviced and it was quick and easy, then the next time it was an unorganized disaster? This is a clear example of a lack of proper systems. The workers just do their best with what they are given and sometimes it works, but most times it does not.

All this piles up and before long the first time business owner starts to think, "Life was better when I didn't have to worry about all of this." They start missing the days when they just had to do their job and go home, and someone else worried about everything. This can be avoided by instituting the correct systems in the beginning. Ideally you would structure your business so it could run without you. You should do this for a few reasons. First, if you're sick, or have to miss a day for personal reasons, or want to take a vacation, business can go on. Next, someday you may want to open another business which would be impossible if you have to be at the initial one all the time. Lastly, if you make great systems and the process is repeatable, you could franchise the business and have others grow it for you.

Creating systems is rather simple. It's the idea of relinquishing control that most struggle with. First time business owners often feel the need to be everywhere all the time. You must fight this urge as it is very damaging to your chances at success. Creating a system could be as easy as typing up a step by step guide for every position in the business, which in the beginning probably won't be many. For example if you open a car wash, you may have a greeter in the beginning of the wash. The system could be: 1. Greet customer with a smile and ask which package they want; 2. Collect funds for chosen package; 3. Rinse outside of car to remove loose debris; 4. Guide customer into wash tunnel. That is given to the employee and explained when they are hired. Now that is a very simple example but the idea is the same from the most entry level position to the most complicated. Perhaps you have a binder in the office that has all the position's systems in it for reference at any time.

When every position knows exactly what to do, and how and when to do it the correct way, and it can be referenced in writing, you increase your chances for success immensely. It is up the supervisor, which could be the business owner, to make sure people are following the systems. Inspect what you expect. I heard that saying years ago and still follow it today. You can have all the systems in the world but if no one is making sure they are being executed they are useless. Create the systems and make sure they are being followed and watch your business run like a well-oiled machine!

Change with the times

Refusing to constantly change, evolve, and improve has brought down many companies. Look at the recent demise of Blockbuster, Oldsmobile, and Kodak to name a few. What do they all have in common? You guessed it, they didn't change with the times. Blockbuster was by far the leading movie rental company. It was extremely successful with thousands of locations all over the country. Then Netflix started mailing movies to people. Then Netflix made it possible to stream movies right to your TV. What did blockbuster do?

Hardly anything. Oldsmobile is another example. They made cars for older people. Then their older clientele base started disappearing as old people will do, and they had no one to fill that sales void. Their volume and profits started shrinking, it was too late to capture a different customer base and after decades in business, it closed its doors. Kodak was thought by many to be the best film for years. Then digital cameras came out. People had less and less need for film. Kodak did not adjust to the new technology and slowly faded away.

These are just a few examples of well known companies that went out of business for failure to change with the times. It's almost sad as many of us have grown up with these companies. It has happened to thousands of other companies too. Our world is constantly changing around us, and in many ways. Technology is advancing faster now more than ever. Customers want everything quicker, cheaper, and better. Employees want to work less and feel more entitled by the day. As a business owner you <u>must</u> be cognizant of this and do what you can to stay ahead of, or at least keep up with the curve.

Don't be discouraged by these examples. Some might say, "If these giant companies went under, what chance do I have?" You have a great chance, just don't rest on your laurels. A business owner must know that their company is there to serve. All companies serve different types of customers, but they all serve. Keeping service the main goal in your company, and constantly trying to serve better, you will be leaps and bounds ahead of others that put profit or volume first and service after. If serving is the main priority your company will constantly be trying to be better, faster, and for a lower price so you won't be keeping up with the times, you will be ahead!

KEY #6

Multiple Streams of Income

The final key to your six-figure income! Discussing multiple streams of income as the last chapter of the book is no accident. It is vital you have the knowledge of the previous 5 keys to really understand and make this happen. More than one income source is so important, not just to help achieve or surpass your six figure income goal, but for overall financial security. It pains me to see families go into financial ruin because the main income earner in the household lost their job. Most of you reading this book have seen this happen before, or even worse perhaps it has happened to you. To rely on the company you work for to essentially pay your bills and put food on the table is frightening, especially in today's workplace where values like loyalty, trust, and honor don't rank anywhere near as high in most companies' eyes as the bottom line does.

When you have at least a few streams of income, if a situation like losing your job does happen, it's not really that big of a deal. In fact you could look at it like time off because your other incomes are still there. Now that is true financial security! When some think of financial security, ideas like pensions, money in the bank, and retirement plans come to mind. If you lose your job, money in the bank starts to dwindle fast, and pensions and retirement plans wont do much for you. It's having other sources of income to fall back on that truly secures your finances.

Multiple income streams are not only good for peace of mind. Having more than one income stream coming in means making more money every month and every year. That means more money to live on, have fun with, and the best part, more money to invest to make more money! See, the problem with most people is once they get a job that pays the bills and leaves a little extra, they become complacent. If this sounds a little too familiar it's okay, it's human nature. However, the fact that you are reading this book means you're not happy with that. You want more than the average Joe or Jane. Think about this: if you establish a second income stream of just $500 a week, (which is not hard at all) that is $26000 more a year. What could you do with that? What does that do to your retirement plan? Or your kids college fund? How fast could you pay your house off applying that to the principle every year? Or maybe you would have fun with it. Buy a boat, motorcycle, or a vacation home. The point of this chapter, and this book for that matter, is not to tell you what to do with your six figures, I just want you to earn it! I hope you will be smart with your money, but that is for another book.

These numbers are very conservative to boot. My second stream of income earned me up to $100k a year, and I had no special skill. It was self-taught, and a lot of work, but eventually I put systems and good people in place and now it runs on about 30 hours a year of my time. We will discuss in this chapter more specifics on how to establish and maintain multiple streams of income, many of which that don't require you to invent a new product or have any other unique skill. Just some focus, hard work, and willingness to make it happen!

Be ready to work

Strategies

There are probably as many ways to develop multiple streams of income as there are waves in the sea. In other words, I'm not going to say "This is the way and the only way." That would be silly. Furthermore, as you have seen in this book, I'm not going to talk about how great it is to have all this money pouring in and not tell you some specific strategies to get it done. My point is, don't get locked in on the examples I am going to give you and think those are the only ways to do it. I only give you some of the ways I have done it to stimulate your thinking, to get the gears in your head working. Just as I said in the first chapter, mindset is the most important part to getting to six figures, it applies to the last chapter just the same.

AAA: You must have the mindset of always being on the lookout for ways to create income and be ready to work for it. It's that simple. Do that and you will develop many income streams.

Just like anything else, it won't happen overnight. This is going to be a lifestyle change in the beginning while you are creating them, and later when you can enjoy them.

This chapter is the perfect follow-up to the chapter on entrepreneurship because many subsequent income streams are entrepreneurial in nature. Moreover, one goes about finding them in the same way an entrepreneur would go about finding their next business opportunity. See what service you could provide, and cash in! You most likely want to look for something you could do while maintaining your full time job. It could be something you do mostly in your off hours after work or on the weekends. Or if you have the type of job where calls and computer work could be done there then that broadens your options even more.

Real Estate

Let's get into some specific examples I have seen work so you know what I mean. Real estate is my favorite by far. There are many different aspects of real estate that can create income for you, but for now we will speak about flipping and rentals. Flipping is a great income generator. It can be done in your off time before and after work, and on weekends. You can be as hands on and involved as you wish. This is the source I mentioned earlier that has provided me with up to $100k a year. I could literally write an entire book on flipping, and I may one day, but for now I'll just go over the basics. You buy a property that is undervalued, typically because it needs some work, fix it up, and sell it for a profit. I'm sure you have seen the shows on TV. Those shows are great, but a word of caution—they may make it look easier than it is. Like anything that can provide you with that type of income, there is much to learn. The good news is you can teach yourself. Go back to chapter four and apply the information in there to house flipping and you can succeed. Rush in thinking you've got it without researching and learning first, and you could find yourself in big trouble. I educated myself for a year before I bought my first investment property.

Another aspect of real estate that provides a great second income is rental properties. This segment is much different than flipping but also has great benefits. The basics to rental success are buy a property, rent it out, and maintain it. This won't give you the big chunks of profit like flipping can provide. You will get a small paycheck every month for every property, but over time, through the property appreciating and paying off the mortgage if you have one, you can build substantial wealth. Plus if you do need a chunk of cash you can sell a property and cash in on the equity. Once you get the property and have a tenant in paying the rent, it is much more hands off than flipping, making it almost a fully passive income. Then, you acquire more and more properties and build up what is called a portfolio, and you could be receiving a substantial income every month from this. Some of the biggest fortunes in the world have been done through this method of real estate. As an investor you can rent out single family homes, multi-family homes from two family duplexes, up to apartment buildings to commercial space. There are many niches in real estate and money can be made in all of them.

Side Business

This is pretty obvious. Start a business you can run 'on the side'. We went over this in detail in the previous chapter so I won't repeat myself, but I will expand a little. If you have an even relatively demanding full time job, you might want to steer towards something that can immediately or eventually be run mostly passively. The reason for this is obvious. If your side business requires you to work full time and you have a full time job, you can't be in two places at once!

If proper systems and people are put in place, most businesses can be run with an absentee owner. However, if you are the whole business then it most likely wouldn't work out. For example if you open a consulting business, meaning you consult or help others in an area in which you are an expert, and it requires your presence most of the day, that is not a side business. For the most part, as long as you plan properly most businesses can be ran in your spare time.

I have seen people buy goods at garage sales and sell them online and do well, and enjoy it. Some are experts in some aspect of home improvement and do that on the weekends. Some examples of that are tile work, landscaping, and renovating kitchens and bathrooms. Some are great with kids and become a nanny for busy parents who need help. Others open brick and mortar stores like convenience stores, liquor stores, car washes, used car lots, and do very well. If you're good with engines you could buy cars, tractors, lawn mowers that aren't working, fix them, and sell them for a great profit. Like I said, these are examples of things I have seen work well as side businesses to stimulate your thinking.

The internet provides a ton of opportunity for side business. As mentioned before, you can buy and sell online in huge marketplaces like eBay and Amazon. Some make videos and post them on YouTube. If you get enough views, companies will pay you to advertise during your videos. Others do very well with online marketing businesses and advertising for others.

The list of things to do on the side to create income goes on forever. Pick something, take a small step each day, and make it happen. You can do it. I believe in you!

Investing

There are many different ways to invest your money to create side income. Especially with the internet, it is all automated now, meaning it can be done from your computer! I know that seems obvious but 20 years before this book was written it was a much more drawn out process. Now you can log on, and in a few clicks invest in almost anything you want.

A favorite for part time investors looking for some extra income is stocks. The idea is simple. Go online and search for stock trading companies. The big ones will pop up on the top of your screen. Choose whichever one you like and make an account. It only takes a few minutes and you're ready to go. Buy stock, it goes up, then you sell it and make money! Huge fortunes have been made in the stock market, but like anything else that gives you the opportunity to make big bucks, you better do your research first or you could lose big bucks.

Some buy and sell stocks multiple times in one day. Others buy and hold for months or years before they sell. Some hold forever and collect what are called dividends that some stocks pay out for side income. You can also contact a stockbroker for advice on investing in stocks. They are highly trained experts who will guide you the best they can to buy the correct stocks, and when to sell also. Like anything else there are good stockbrokers and bad ones, so maybe ask your friends and family for recommendations.

Authoring

Most people have some knowledge about something that is worth writing about. So why not share that knowledge and get paid for it? In today's high tech world, becoming an author is much easier than it once was. Years ago you would write a book and beg a publisher to just read it, never mind actually publish it. Now you can self-publish and sell it online. Virtually anyone can become an author, why not you? What are you good at? What advice do you have to give? What story do you have to tell? I believe most people have a book in them. Whether it's an experience they went through, a point of view they want to get across, or a special skill they want to help others with; you have something. Once again, don't try to sit down and write a book, that's way too daunting. Instead, take small steps every day, like just 500 words. Then another 500 the next day. Most find that the writing comes easier than expected, and it is quite therapeutic.

Furthermore, because of today's technology, writing a book isn't your only option. Many get paid very well for writing for websites. Others write on a blog, or start their own. There are successful blogs about virtually everything. Some blogs that come to mind are cooking, financial, how-to, relationships, religion, and lifestyle. Then as you get more people visiting your blog your visitor count goes up. The higher the visitor count gets, the more companies will pay you to advertise on your blog. Ta da! Side income from writing about something you are knowledgeable in, and you don't even have to leave your bed!

Some of you are saying, "I don't even know how to type, I could never make a living writing." Well thanks to modern technology you don't have to know how to type. There are programs where you just talk into a device and it does the typing for you. On that note however, learning to type is actually pretty easy, and once you can do it stays with you, almost like riding a bike, as long as you do it somewhat frequently. There are great free programs online that teach you how to type like a pro. Some are in game form so it's fun at the same time. Use those programs every day for 20 minutes and in a couple weeks you will be a typing master!

Now What?

Since you just read approximately 2500 words on creating multiple streams of income, now your brain is working on it. Without you even knowing it your mind is beginning to think about different ways you could perhaps create some income streams of your own. However, just reading this chapter isn't going to be enough. Now it's mind programming time—like we discussed in chapter 2.

AAA: Every day you must spend some time thinking about what your next move will be in getting some other income streams going. I recommend in the morning, but whenever you can dedicate ten or more minutes to it is fine. That time is to be spent brainstorming. Whether it's writing down any idea that comes to your head on a piece of paper, or thinking out loud to yourself about ideas. If you are having trouble coming up with ideas, look around at people you know. What do they do for a living, on the side? Look around your town. What is missing, or what is there that you could do better, or for less?

Don't get frustrated if you can't come up with something right away. Just keep dedicating ten or so minutes a day to it and keep your eyes open where ever you go. I guarantee you will come up with a great idea. Remember, if the first or second idea doesn't work, keep trying. Failure is simply finding out what doesn't work, and gets you one step closer to finding out what does. Develop those streams, even if they are little, because many little streams make a big river.

CLOSING

Congratulations! You have come to the end. You now know the 6 keys to attaining a six-figure income. Writing this book has been a truly great experience for me. One of the reasons it has been so rewarding is because I know that this book, if acted upon, will change the lives of so many in such a positive way. That doesn't make me happy because I am trying to take credit; I'm simply happy if the change occurs, period. I live the six-figure income life and have for many years now. I know how it can help form a foundation for a great life. I am also familiar with a life of not making six figures, without abundance, where you may be right now.

The vast majority of people today live in debt just to get by. Your life does not have to be like that. You can turn it around, but you *must* be willing to change. By change I don't mean your values or principles, I mean your thinking, habits, and behavior. Most people are programmed for negativity and mediocrity when they are capable of so much more. I am asked almost daily by friends, family, and employees how I do it. How do I run all these businesses, stay in shape, raise two kids, and still have a ton of fun? My answers used to be all different for all the different people. Now the answer is simple— read my book.

It's all in here. All the practices and principles I have used over the years to create a life of extra: extra money, respect, love, time, health, and fun. This book could have easily been five times longer. I tried my absolute best to make it compact and easy to read because I feel that is important in today's culture of immediate gratification. I know that sometimes it's not easy to motivate yourself to read a 500-page book. It's a daunting task for some, and that is not what I wanted for this book. This is a manuscript full of actionable advice you can put to use immediately. I wish you the absolute best in life and I hope this book will help you get it!

www.ingramcontent.com/pod-product-compliance
Lightning Source LLC
Chambersburg PA
CBHW071313220526
45468CB00001B/359